BOOKS

THAT ALL CHILDREN
SHOULD HEAR AND READ

PERPETUATING THE STORIES

BOOKS

THAT ALL CHILDREN SHOULD HEAR AND READ

PERPETUATING THE STORIES

Cherie A. Clodfelter, PhD

BROWN BOOKS
PUBLISHING GROUP

BOOKS
THAT ALL CHILDREN SHOULD HEAR AND READ
PERPETUATING THE STORIES

Manufactured in the United States of America.

For Information, please contact:

Brown Books Publishing Group
16200 North Dallas Parkway, Suite 170
Dallas, Texas 75248
www.brownbooks.com
972-381-0009

A New Era in Publishing™

Cover artwork by Chelsea Davis.

Interior illustrations by Elizabeth Fisher.

ISBN-13: 978-1-934812-16-7
ISBN-10: 1-934812-16-1
LCCN: 2008932014

1 2 3 4 5 6 7 8 9 10

Table of Contents

Introductory Materials

**Books that All Children Should Hear and Read:
Perpetuating the Stories**
By Cherie A. Clodfelter, PhD

Special note to all readers about the publication of and proceeds from the sale of Books that All Children Should Hear and Read: Perpetuating the Stories.

I would personally like to offer my sincere thanks to Colleen and Frank Trabold, who generously contributed all of the funds necessary for the publication of *Books that All Children Should Hear and Read: Perpetuating the Stories*. Their generous contribution allows all proceeds from the sale of this book to go directly into the Dr. Cherie A. Clodfelter Scholarship fund that benefits prospective elementary teachers during their student teaching semester. Colleen Trabold came to the University of Dallas for one semester, Spring 2007. In that one semester, she experienced the impact of Dr. Clodfelter. Her generous contribution to this publication stands as a testament to the influence of good teachers and to the power of good stories.

—Barbara Khirallah, Editor

To order more copies of this book in support of the Cherie A. Clodfelter Scholarship, please see the ordering information at the end of the book.

Foreword
Dr. Richard P. Olenick

Cherie A. Clodfelter & Dr. Richard P. Olenick

*E*ach of us has the opportunity to shape the lives of those around us. For most of us, we impact the lives of our brothers and sisters, parents, and friends. Occasionally, an individual can influence the lives of a greater number of people through hard work and persistence. Truly exceptional, however, is the individual who can influence an entire community or a city. Such an individual is Dr. Cherie Clodfelter, who now spreads her influence from the Dallas-Fort Worth Metroplex to the nation with the publication of *Books that All Children Should Hear and Read: Perpetuating the Stories*. Contained within its pages are gems from children's literature on which Cherie shares her insights.

I've seen how Cherie has shaped and nurtured hundreds of future teachers. I've even calculated that in her tenure at the University of Dallas she has supervised the development of 2,386 anthologies, guided 1,408 student-authored children's literature books, and driven 46,620 miles to visit and nurture student teachers. That last figure is almost twice around the earth! Cherie not only goes out of her way for students, she goes around the world! Of course, to look at her contribution in terms of numbers would miss the essence of her work with children's literature.

At a time when children are over-scheduled and unduly stressed, parents should ask themselves what roles literature can play in their children's lives. Acquaintances with characters in books mold the first ways a child has of making sense of what being human means. Children—and adults alike—come to know more clearly who and what they are while exploring imaginatively what they might become through characters in stories. While hearing a story or reading one, a child begins to inhabit the world of the story and through awe comes to know both his/herself and the world. The events of a story and the characters depicted provide a means for exploring the world that helps a child to reinforce, to illuminate, and to relate to his or her own experiences. Story gives public form to private meanings and thus helps those who receive its messages to reach out to other human beings in the world, knowing that they share some of the same concerns and feelings. We all need to learn about life both literally and literarily.

Cherie reacquaints us with classics such as the magic and bewilderment of *A Wrinkle in Time* or the morals in *The Ugly Duckling*. She reminds us of historical figures that have shaped our lives such as *The Life and Death of Crazy Horse*. And she delights in reminding us of the meaning of friendship found in *Charlotte's Web*.

In *The Unwritten*, W.S. Merwin wrote
> Inside this pencil
> crouch words that have never been written
> never been spoken
> never been taught
> they're hiding

In her book, Cherie sheds light on the words and ideas that are hiding within each child. She offers a lifetime of insights that will help parents and teachers select stories that form children and help them grow. Her leadership has always been a voice of balance, harmony, and good sense. She speaks her mind and her convictions even when what she has to say may be unpopular or something others do not wish to hear. She is always direct, to the point, and incisive in her readings of a situation. When asked, "What do you make?" she will respond within a heartbeat, "I make a difference." *Books that All Children Should Hear and Read: Perpetuating the Stories* will make a difference in the lives of your children.

(Editor's Note: Dr. Richard P. Olenick currently is professor of physics at The University of Dallas where he holds the Nancy Cain Marcus and Jeffrey A. Marcus Chair in Science. Owner of four beautiful Borzoi, Dr. Olenick, like his good friend Cherie Clodfelter, "knows his dogs." He is a popular teacher of physics and astronomy courses and has worked with high school teachers for twenty years on such projects as the PBS series The Mechanical Universe and C3P—The Comprehensive Conceptual Curriculum for Physics. He has directed numerous grants from the National Science Foundation and the U.S. Department of Education and received many awards, including a CASE Texas Professor of the Year in 1995 and Piper Professor of 1997 from the Minnie Stevens Piper Foundation.)

BOOKS

THAT ALL CHILDREN SHOULD HEAR AND READ

PERPETUATING THE STORIES

Cherie A. Clodfelter, PhD

"Know Your Dogs"

A Meaningful Philosophy of Education

Cherie A. Clodfelter

*M*y philosophy of education, as so much in my life, comes from listening and thinking about what others say combined with my own thoughts.

When I graduated from college, I had a perfectly wonderful philosophy of education: it had a little Dewey, a little Plato, a little Piaget. It was really beautifully written and could be articulated beautifully as well. But it just wasn't me—although it was all truly felt; it was all form and not substance that goes to the heart. My philosophy, one which I could readily express in simple, meaningful language, came from an experience with a little boy who lived on my cul-de-sac. His name was Mike, and he was eight years old. He often came over to my house to play with my miniature schnauzer because he didn't have a dog. His father had promised that he could have a dog as soon as he could handle the responsibilities—whenever that meant!

Around Thanksgiving, Mike came to visit, and he had with him a precious puppy, Maude. Mike explained that his daddy had given him the dog early for Christmas since he had learned how to handle responsibilities! Now, this puppy jumped up on you, barked up a storm, and paid no heed to Mike. In short, the puppy was unlearned, uneducated, and didn't know how to behave at all. I did not see Mike again in person until around early March. He had Maude with him. Maude sat down when Mike told her to do so. She looked affectionately at Mike, ready to obey his every command. In four short months, Maude had become a most well-behaved dog—and her obedience showed her training, showed that she had become a *learned* dog. I asked Mike how he had done it. What Mike said to me then helped me to express exactly what I believe about education. Mike explained, 'Well, I knew what I wanted my dog to learn, I tried to find out how she could learn it best, and I know my dog awful well!'

From that day forward, everyone who knows me—especially young, prospective teachers—hears this story and understands my philosophy of education simply as "Know your dogs!" That is teaching!

Children's Literature: A Personal Heritage
by Cherie Clodfelter

*I*t can't be thirty years! Has it really been thirty years since I started working with children and young adults and the literature written especially for them?

Can you imagine the privilege of recovering children's literature as an adult? What a joy this has been! What was the beginning? I know in my heart and soul this great adventure had its inspiration in my heritage, my own childhood: A heritage filled with "when-I-was-a-little-boy" stories from my father and the love of "this is a really good story" from my mother. I, of course, have to include stories from my two grandfathers, who were pioneers in Indian Territory before Oklahoma became the forty-sixth state. Their stories were exciting and mysterious, with themes of "the good prevails and the right receive their rewards."

Mother, Father, Granddads Clodfelter and Goyer, Aunt Mittie, Uncle Polly, and the environment of the pioneer spirit of the 1940s and 1950s helped to create my matrix—on which I am still building. No one could have been more blessed with the feel of the "story."

As a child and later as an adult, I came to understand the impact of story. I connected with others through the stories that were told and the stories that we lived. Stories created relationships . . . as in the biblical stories of Joseph and his brothers, David and Solomon, and the parables told by Jesus. In these stories I saw good and bad, and I established within myself my traditions, my connections, my standards, and the importance of both sadness and joy. The "characters" in stories created the mosaic, the inlaid design of who I am, my hopes and dreams for the future. Making decisions based on "the little inner voice" came as much from my "real" family as from both the rounded characters and the minor characters in my stories. I still hear the voices of all these people in my being, in my soul, in my life.

What a glorious heritage for me, for anyone! The tradition of tales coming alive through the voice of the storyteller, out of the pages of a special book is the gift of children's and young adults' literature. The human voice must remain and can be "heard" when a child listens to both prose and poetry with the master storyteller—the author that has the gift of storytelling.

When I was asked to create an annotated list of books that I felt had a lasting impact on both the child and the adult reader, I thought: what fun, a collection of classics. After all, my career of the past thirty years has been to collect stories . . . as a teacher, as a storyteller, as a reviewer. Oh, but it is not so simple, so easy to decide the classics. What are my criteria, my standards, my points of reference for such a group of so-called classics in children's literature?

Thus, let me begin at the beginning . . . with some definitions.

What is children's literature? The literature for children is an aesthetic experience based upon the child's ability to toy with words and concepts. It incorporates feelings, emotions, desires, and needs that will allow the reader/listener to interact with and to relive the story and pictures again and again. An extension of experiences constructed from previous experiences or the creation of new ideas from the long ago past or the far ahead future are crucial elements in children's literature. The imagination of a child allows the freedom to soar in a way that reflects a part of what childhood should be: a passion for the power of knowing and the thrill of living. The literature for children, along with the illustrations to illuminate the depth of that literature, gives a special time when the child can perceive vicariously with humor, beauty, wonder, along with despair, ugliness, and sorrow.

Too lengthy? I agree. The definition above is for the adult.

What is the child's definition? "It lets me imagine; it lets me play-like and doesn't tell me what to think. I'm not asked what the author meant 'cause I don't know the guy. It is a book that I want to read over—maybe not all the book, but part of it because I really like it. I find lots of new things every time I hear it or read it."

I really believe in the adult definition of children's literature, yet I "like" the child's definition.

Frances C. Sayers in *Summoned by Books* (1965) writes,
> We all have, in our experience,
> memories of certain books which
> changed us in some way—by disturbing
> us, or by a glorious affirmation of some
> emotion we knew but could never shape
> in words, or by some revelation of
> human nature.[1]

Virginia Woolf calls such times "moments of being."

The element of endurance is an issue in selecting "classics." Time cannot be the single most important ingredient. Time cannot be the judge of books for children. The child has a limited time frame for judging the impact of a book on himself or herself. A book that is all-engrossing and lifts the spirit is a classic. Children are quick to judge, and that first impression is long lasting. Whether written a hundred years ago or last year, the book becomes a personal experience, and that personal response creates a classic for the child.

Jean Karl in her book, *From Childhood to Childhood* (1970), writes,

> A book that is alive clings to the
> reader and gives him a sense of
> belonging to it, or at best, a sense of
> witnessing events that are really
> taking place. . . .The book that lives
> makes itself seem important because
> it relates to life itself.[2]

The power of story is not to be denied. In prehistoric caves, in pilgrim settlements, in Cherokee lodges, in Nazi concentration camps, stories were as important as food. They were sometimes served instead, and they nourished starving hearts.

Who are the children connected to the children's literature? Chronologically, they are from the newborn or infant to the thirteen-year-old. I often refer to the eleven-to-thirteen-year-old crowd as "bridge kids." Bridge kids seek books with multi-themes closer to the literature for the young adult. Notice I have not mentioned grade level, and I will not. One of the beauties of children's literature is that it has never been "graded" even though there are those who, for their own convenience, have attempted to do so . . . with lists such as "fourth-grade books." I am ashamed of these individuals.

I was teaching seven- and eight-year-olds in a second-grade public school classroom in Irving, Texas. Shelley, a precocious child with a shorter-than-average physical frame, was attempting to check out E. B. White's *Charlotte's Web* from the school librarian. "You are not in third grade, Shelley. Besides, you are too little, and you are not old enough to read it with understanding," stated the librarian. But Shelley persisted: "Are you sure you won't let me check it out, Mrs. Walker? There is some really good stuff in there."

Shelley came from a rich background of being read to, and she herself was reading long before she came to school. What an ignorant librarian! The ending to the story? I gave Shelley her own paperback copy of *Charlotte's Web*. A second ending—I have heard from Shelley for the past twenty years. She is a surgeon with a husband and two children. Her favorite book is still *Charlotte's Web*, and both of her children have their own paperback copies of her favorite book.

Ninety-six books for children make up my collection. Impossible! Nevertheless, I have attempted to comment on each of these, my classics. The books are arranged by genre: picture books, fiction, information books and biographies, traditional literature (folktales, myths, poetry, parables, fables, legends, tall tales), and fantasy and science fiction. There may be an imbalance in the collection, and I do not apologize for this imbalance. It is my list!

A second disclaimer: The narrative to accompany each selection is in the same style as I utilized in the introduction to the collection. My thoughts and feelings about the entries are mine. I have spoken about them not as a critic; rather I speak from my experiences that join child and story, mind and heart. After all, one reads with the heart as well as the mind. Each book has quality of writing, yet much more, and it is the "much more," I feel, that makes it a book or story to be heard and then heard and read again and again.

Notes
[1] Sayers, Frances. *Summoned by Books*. New York: Viking Press, 1965.
[2] Karl, Jean. *From Childhood to Childhood*. New York: John Day Company, 1970.

Picture Books

Allard, Harry
Miss Nelson Is Missing!
Houghton Mifflin, 1985. Illustrated by James Marshall.

Children would never forgive me if Miss Nelson were not on my list of classic books. The story is ridiculous, yet it produces belly laughs among children. Everyone but the authors seems to know who the substitute teacher for Miss Nelson really is. What a hoot!

Anno, Mitsumasa
Anno's USA
Philomel Books, 1983.

The Asian artist and author Anno became so enamored with America that he created this chronological history of the United States backwards! His little rider comes in from California and travels across the broad expanse. As he arrives on the east coast, he sees the Mayflower coming over the horizon. This is a super book with all types of historical and literary characters embedded in the land. For instance, Raggedy Ann and Andy are on the plains; Max and the Wild Things are in a New York parade; Virginia Burton's Little House is in a forest; and even Charlie Chaplin dances in New Orleans. Every time you pick up this wordless picture book, you find another well-known character. I think this is a fabulous book for children in the upper grades. You must have some knowledge of American history fully to appreciate its fun.

Baker, Olaff
Where the Buffaloes Begin
Puffin, 1985. Illustrated by Stephen Gammell.

"Over the blazing camp fires, when the wind moaned eerily through the thickets of juniper and fir, they spoke of it in the Indian tongue—of the strange lake to the south whose water never rests. Nawa, the wise man, declared 'that if you arrive at the right time, on the right night, you would see the buffaloes begin.'" These are the beginning lines of a book so sensory you almost hear and smell the buffaloes. The tale of Little Wolf, a courageous boy who longs to find the lake that his grandfather tells about, is dramatic. Early one morning, Little Wolf heads south on an adventure to find where the buffaloes begin. The narrative is bold and strong. Gammell's drawings are unforgettable.

Barron, T. A.
Where Is Grandpa?
Penguin Young Readers Group, 2000.
Illustrated by Chris K. Soentpiet.

The hardest question asked by a child when a loved one dies is where they have gone. It is most often explained as "being called home." Then why are so many crying? When Barron's father died, he had to talk to his children about Grandpa's death. This book grew out of the experience. Barron does his explaining with directness, sensitivity, and compassion. And in all of the explaining, there is honesty and simplicity. "Where were you with Grandpa? . . . There he will always be with you in your adventures and memories." What a glorious concept!

Bunting, Eve
The Wall
Clarion Books, 1992. Illustrated by Ronald Himler.

The author and illustrator have created in *The Wall* a beautifully told and illustrated story of the Vietnam conflict from a child's point of view. The simple tale takes place at the Memorial in Washington, D.C. Told in first person, the story describes how the little boy is taken by his father to the Vietnam Wall to find the name of his grandfather who perished in the conflict. The sequence of events culminates when they find the name they are seeking. This is truly how a child should remember the terrible conflict. The watercolor drawings are double page and so realistic. Even if you have been to the Wall, you will be startled with this book's impact on you.

dePaola, Tomie
Tomie dePaola's Mother Goose
G.P. Putnam's Sons, 1985.

The well-loved Mother Goose rhymes are delightfully presented in the typical "pillow people" style of dePaola. Children adore the rhymes and illustrations. DePaola has written and illustrated some of the most sought after stories, folktales, and realistic fiction children could ever want. This large volume of Mother Goose could have been listed under traditional literature. I chose to list it under picture books because of the impact the illustrations make on the rhymes.

Geisel, Theodore (Dr. Seuss)
The Cat in the Hat
Random House Books for Young Readers, 1957.

What started out for Geisel as a linguistic reader has turned into the most recognizable cat throughout the world. The story is nonsense, the beloved cat is absurd, yet no child can resist the antics of the Cat and his Hat. The vivid Geisel illustrations charm children every-where. My favorite Geisel poem is "Marco Comes Late," but it is very hard to find. It's worth seeking.

Henkes, Kevin
Owen
Greenwillow, 1993.

Is there another author or artist who writes and draws so faithfully from the child's perspective? I doubt it. Henkes deals with problems all children experience in one form or another. Owen, Henkes' mouse protagonist, cannot give up Fuzzy, his blanket, and he will be attending kindergarten soon. The nosy next-door neighbor gives Owen's parents lots of advice on how to get rid of Fuzzy. The text never makes fun of Owen and thus does not make fun of the reader/listener. The watercolor drawings are appealing in their bright colors. You will love Owen!

Henkes, Kevin
Chrysanthemum
Greenwillow, 1991.

Chrysanthemum has the most special, outstanding, glorious name in the world. Her mother and daddy tell her that it is "absolutely perfect." However, when Chrysanthemum starts school, her new friends make fun of her name and tease her because she is named for a flower. Poor, poor Chrysanthemum! Her life becomes miserable until the new music teacher changes the entire situation. The wonderful illustrations respond to each and every mood of the text. "Chrysanthemum, Chrysanthemum, Chrysanthemum!"

Kitchen, Bert
Animal Alphabet
Dial, 1984.

These are not the usual animals found around a classroom to represent letters in the alphabet. No, sir! These are strange, wonderful creatures done in huge dimensions, often in double page spreads. Using black and white drawings, Kitchen makes the animals seem more alive. (A list of the animals is on the final pages.)

Leaf, Munro
The Story of Ferdinand
Viking Press, 1963. Illustrated by Robert Lawson.

Very young children receive their initial experiences with reading through pictures. They "read" the illustrations while an adult reads the writing. "Oh, this is what those scribble marks are all about," they exclaim. The illustrations create pictures of meaning in the minds of children. Thus the importance of picture books cannot be diminished in the life and future of young children. Ferdinand is an outstanding example of matching the reading of pictures and the reading of words. The pictures of the little black and white bull sitting peacefully under his cork tree and later among the flowers of the bullring are captivating to children. Ferdinand does not want to worry his mother, a cow, but he doesn't want to be the most ferocious bull in all of Spain. He wants only to smell the flowers and enjoy the peace of the pasture.

Lionni, Leo
Frederick's Fables:
A Treasury of 16 Favorite Leo Lionni Stories
Pantheon Books, 1985.

Frederick, the mouse, tells the Aesop fables in a mouse-like manner that intrigues the very young. The modern vernacular seems to work well. The episodes are faithful to the original fables and perhaps have greater meaning for the child. The collage artwork encourages the child to touch and feel the pages.

Lobel, Arnold
Frog and Toad Are Friends
Harper & Row, 1970.

Need more be said? The Laurel and Hardy of the amphibian world
have conversations that are priceless! The dialogue is rich and believ-
able. Lobel is a master at creating understated humorous interchanges
between the two friends. The tiny ink drawings are expressive and
detailed. What a treat!

Moore, Clement C.
The Night Before Christmas
Putnam Publishing Group, 1998. Illustrated by Jan Brett.

In the 1890s, Clement Moore changed the Santa Claus legend forever
with this classic poem written especially for two little neighborhood
girls. Santa is real, he rewards good children, and he is magical. With
fabulous illustrations of Brett, circled with lavish and detailed borders, this edition has become my favorite of many versions of "T'was
the night before Christmas and all through the house. . . ."

Piper, Watty
The Little Engine That Could
Platt & Munk, 1954 (1930).
Illustrated by George and Doris Hauman.

Young children appreciate anthropomorphism, especially in inani-
mate objects such as toys and machines. This may be the fascination
found in the little engine that pulled the boxcars of toys over the
mountain with sheer determination. The illustrations are horrid! The
"I think I can, I thought I could, I knew I could" is the joy.

Potter, Beatrix
The Tale of Peter Rabbit
Fredrick Warne & Co., 1902. (The collection of twenty-four books.)

I could cry for the child who does not hear the stories of Peter Rabbit and all his friends. Potter's light and delicate watercolors add just the right touch to these timeless tales. The rabbit Peter is a scamp, as are his assorted companions. I have voice tapes of a British visiting professor at the University of Dallas reading the Tales. "Pettar" sounds terrific in British English dialect.

Rey, H. A.
Curious George
Arranged by Houghton Mifflin,
published by Scholastic Bookservices, 1941.

Oh, to be like George and have one escapade after another! The comical monkey's antics are exciting, rather dangerous. The Man with the Yellow Hat always saves the day so George can get on with what all children wish they could do.

Sciezka, Jon
The True Story of the 3 Little Pigs
Viking Kestral, 1989. Illustrated by Lane Smith

I almost did not include Sciezka's fractured Grimm story in my list, but then I thought of the rolling-on-the-floor-with-laughter behavior of children when they have heard/read the real story of those three little porkers. The humor is extended by A. Wolf himself, as he writes the true story. A child told me not to read this book when I was hungry because hamburgers, a cake, and lots of sugar were in the story! The clever use of paradox cannot be ignored, and children recognize this style of writing with glee.

Sendak, Maurice
Where the Wild Things Are
Harper & Row, 1963.

Max is a mischievous little boy with a huge imagination. Once, when his mother called him "a wild thing," he told her he would eat her up. Well, that was all it took for her to send him to his room without supper. Did that thwart Max? Certainly not! He goes to where the wild things are, and he becomes their beloved king. "Let the rumpus begin!" In time, Max longs for home, so he tells the wild things he must go, and he does. Of course, you know where his supper is when he gets home. The art is the focal point in this masterpiece. The paintings are in Henri Rousseau's French primitive style. Max with his almost sneering smile and the big, ludicrous beasts with their "terrible eyes and terrible teeth" can only be Sendak. Children have a childhood right to be scared—a "dive under the covers" fright—but they must not be terrorized. There is a scare in *Where the Wild Things Are*, but there is terror in Sendak's *Outside Over There*. Be careful!

Steig, William
Sylvester and the Magic Pebble
Windmill Books/Simon & Schuster, 1969.

Steig's luxuriant use of language and superb watercolor illustrations make Sylvester my favorite picture book (at least at this moment in time). The words of picture books are as important as the illustrations; they support children and their desire to use "big words." Steig does not oversimplify, and he does not talk down to children. They must come up to him.

In Sylvester, as in all his other marvelous books, Steig tells a tale of wishes granted to the sorrow of the protagonist. Sylvester Duncan, the little donkey, is every child who has ever lived. He finds a red pebble that he learns is magic. It grants wishes. When Sylvester is not using good sense, he wishes he were a rock on Strawberry Hill, and sure enough he becomes a rock on Strawberry Hill. His family searches frantically for him with no success. Then by coincidence—which often is the case in fiction—Sylvester is reunited with his family. I might add here, *Sylvester and the Magic Pebble* is one of the most often banned picture books. Bet you can't understand why some "wide-eyed psychologists" think the book is not suitable for children.

Turkle, Brinton
Thy Friend, Obadiah
The Viking Press, 1969.

The Starbuck family is Quaker, and they speak as Quakers. "Thy, thee, thou" are common in their conversations. They live on Nantucket Island. Obadiah has a seagull that follows him around, much to his displeasure. His brother and sisters tease him about it, so Obadiah throws a rock at the seagull, and the bird disappears. Obadiah looks for him and seems rather sad when the gull isn't following him. Obadiah finally sees him on the wharf with a large fishhook and line dangling from his beak. "Serves thee right for stealing," says Obadiah. "If thou will let me, I will remove the hook from thy beak." The seagull soars away into the sky. That night, Obadiah's mother says, "Come to the window, Obadiah. Isn't that thy seagull outside?" Sure enough, there he is, feathers ruffled against the wind.

Turkle's glowing illustrations are magnificent. They beautifully depict the story of long ago when a little boy is wrapped in the love of his family and his friend, his gull. Turkle was raised as a Quaker, and that influence is seen and heard in this very special story.

Van Allsburg, Chris
The Polar Express
Houghton Mifflin, 1985.

Many (including me) have said that *The Polar Express* is the first original story of Santa Claus since Clement Moore wrote his narrative poem, "Twas the Night Before Christmas" in the early twentieth century. Van Allsburg's illustrations are stunning. The rhythm in the narrative is reflected in the dimly shrouded illustrations. (Van Allsburg seldom uses color in his art; however, this is one of the exceptions.) Children enjoy fantasy, especially if it is read aloud. The mysterious snowy pictures, inside and outside the train, intrigue even the adult. This story cries to be read aloud. Do you ponder the need to still hear the Christmas bell? I do.

Viorst, Judith
Alexander and the Terrible, Horrible, No Good, Very Bad Day
Simon & Schuster: Atheneum, 1972. Illustrated by Ray Cruz.

This is a highly creative story, told in first person by Alexander, about a day when everything goes wrong. He wakes up with gum in his hair, he has lima beans for supper, there is kissing on television, and he gets soap in his eyes. When he announces that he is going to move to Australia, his mom tells him, "Some days are like that. Even in Australia." The child understands these events because most children have experienced similar dilemmas. The charcoal drawings are real! The text carries the color of the story in a surprising way without making fun of Alexander's very real unhappiness.

Ward, Lynd
The Biggest Bear
Houghton Mifflin, 1952.

Ward develops the drama of *The Biggest Bear* in the growth of Johnny's bear. When Johnny first finds his bear, the bear is an adorable, lovable, slightly mischievous cub. The remarkable growth of the cub as he creates chaos throughout the farm suggests the passage of time in a most subtle manner. Near the conclusion of the story, children gasp when they see the gigantic bear gorging himself on the McLeans' maple syrup. The climax also shows growth in Johnny since he takes on the responsibility of making sure the bear does not return to the farm.

The sepia pictures create the sense of adventure with humor and compassion. One thing I have noticed since first reading the story to children in the 1960s is that the child's attitude regarding the "goodness" of the conclusion has changed. Men searching for a big, big bear for their circus capture Johnny's bear. The men are thrilled with the bear, and they assure Johnny he can come and visit the bear. This psychology of capturing animals to perform in a circus is not as pleasant as it once was. Just be aware that you may need to have a discussion about zoos and circus animals with your listeners.

Wagner, Jenny
John Brown, Rose and the Midnight Cat
Bradbury, 1977. Illustrated by Ron Brooks.

In double-page spreads done in magnificent, sensory crosshatch drawings, Brooks has created an expressive companion to a sensitive text. Each time I read the book to children, they are compelled to touch and feel the drawings. Rose is a round-shaped widow. She lives with her huge English sheepdog, John Brown. One night Rose sees something move in the garden. It is a cat the color of midnight.

Rose leaves milk out each night for the cat, and John Brown tips the milk out of the bowl. Rose announces one morning that she is sick and is not going to get up all day. John Brown begins to think that the midnight cat might make Rose feel better. Sure enough, when John Brown lets the midnight cat in the house, Rose gets up, and they all sit by the fire. I love this story and especially the illustrations for their soft appeal to the reader/listener. Jealousy is such a part of childhood and the life of John Brown. Jealousy must be resolved, and John Brown's jealousy is resolved because of his love for Rose.

Yarbrough, Camille
Cornrows
Coward, McCann & Geoghegan. 1979. Illustrated by Carole Byard.

Did you know that in some societies, the culture's history is revealed in the hairstyles? It is true. Yarbrough develops with sensitivity what is "told" in cornrows. The tellers are great-grandmother and mother. As they braid the hair of Sister and her brother Me Too, they sing in rhythmic praise all that cornrow hair has symbolized in the past. Sister names her hairstyle after Langston Hughes, and Me Too names his after Batman. The pride in culture is very strong in the text and in the super, sweeping charcoal illustrations. Warmth, love, and caring for family come through in the connection and importance of heritage.

Yashima, Taro (Jun Iwamatsu, pseudo.)
Crow Boy
Viking, 1955.

In a wonderfully sensitive, definitely Oriental style, Yashima tells the story of Chibi, a young, shy boy from the far away mountains of China. Chibi walks miles to school every day for six years. When he graduates, he has perfect attendance. Yet, he is still lonely and afraid of the other children and especially the old schoolmaster. Chibi's isolation and intense feelings of loneliness continue until the arrival of a friendly schoolmaster who discovers Chibi's talent of imitating crows. Chibi, the teacher finds, knows happy crows from angry crows and mean crows from pleasant crows. The new schoolmaster encourages Chibi to share his knowledge. The children are delighted and give Chibi a new and honored name, Crow Boy. While the illustrations are nondescript and lacking in depth, the story is beautiful and remains forever in one's mind.

Young, Ed
Seven Blind Mice
Philomel, 1992.

As a child I loved to hear my mother read the East Indian fable of the blind man and the elephant. Young retells the fable from the perspective of seven blind mice. The large, empty, black space is filled with what is perceived to be the different shapes of the elephant. The viewer, the child, is mystified by the shapes, as are the mice. Only when the shapes come together on a final double-page spread is the elephant recognized. The striking, bold basic colors represent the different mice. The collage style is awesome in the drama and suspense of the story. Ed Young is one of the premier artists illustrating children's books.

Fiction

Alcott, Louisa May
Little Women
Grossett & Dunlap, 1947.

Meg, Jo, Beth, and Amy live in the time of the Civil War. This background is subtle but never far from the lives of these little women. There is vitality and joy and real life devoid of the sentimentality common at the time. If you are a female, which little woman are you?

Armstrong, William H.
Sounder
Harper & Row, 1969.

Sad dog stories really have a negative influence on me; nevertheless, *Sounder* must be included in my list of classics. Armstrong is a master author who, with tenderness and empathy, creates a story about man's cruel treatment of fellow human beings. This is one of the most moving stories ever. It is a stark and dark tale of a black sharecropper and his family who endure injustice with pride, dignity, and courage. The father is thrown into jail for stealing food for his starving family. His huge hunting dog, Sounder, is cruelly wounded by the sheriff. The dog doesn't bay again until years later when his master returns. Armstrong's novel will remind you of the journey of Odysseus and the faithfulness of Penelope. This would be a story with unbearable despair, except for the fact that a kind and sensitive schoolmaster enlarges the boy's world through education. Be sure you read Armstrong's introduction, or preface, to the story. It is magnificent.

Beatty, Patricia
Charlie Skedaddle
Troll Communications, 1996.

Charley Quinn is one of the Bowery Boys, the toughest street gang in New York City. He loves a good scrap. After his older brother is killed at Gettysburg, this feisty boy vows revenge. He smuggles aboard a troop ship headed for Virginia to enlist as a drummer boy in the Union army. He can't wait until his first battle when he will be responsible for blowing the battle bugle. But when it comes time to blow that cry, the horrors of war and its reality repulses him. Charley "skedaddles." He runs to the mountains to hide from both the Union Army he has deserted and the Confederate Army who will arrest him as a spy. In the mountains of Virginia, he meets Granny Bent. The ornery, secretive old woman helps Charley prove to himself that he is far from being a coward. A powerful story.

Beatty, Patricia
Wait for Me, Watch for Me, Eula Bee
William Morrow, 1978.

The Texas frontier during the time of the war between the states provided such adventure and excitement. Lewallen is the "man of the house" after his father and older brother ride off to join the Confederate army. Lewallen Colliar must look after his mother, old uncle, younger brother, and three-year-old sister, Eula Bee. What a responsibility for a thirteen-year-old! The Comanches attack the homestead, and by the time Lewallen gets back to the cabin, all are lying dead except Eula Bee, and she is no place to be found. Lewallen decides that the Comanches, probably fascinated by her red curls, have taken her captive. He remembers that his mother had always told him that a very young child captured by the Indians becomes Indian. Aware that he and Eula Bee are the only Colliars left, he struggles to find her.

Many months pass before Lewallen (Lutie) finds her among the Indians. Eula Bee does not know him—she has forgotten him and who she is. She kicks, struggles, and screams when Lewallen carries her away. He wonders whether Eula Bee will ever remember him or remember who she is. One day, long after they have returned to the Colliar homestead, Lutie whistles the song "Lorena," which he used to whistle to Eula Bee as a baby. When she says "Lutie" to him, he knows that she has finally remembered. This is a fast moving, quick-paced, and exciting novel where the reader experiences the bonds of the family. The conclusion of the story is satisfying, without being sugary sweet.

Blume, Judy
Are You There God? It's Me, Margaret
Bradbury Press, 1970.

An issue in categorizing literature relates to its appropriateness for a specific chronological age. Realistic fiction is most often thought of for the eleven-to thirteen-year-old. Yet if you have spent time with this age group, you have surely noticed the wide ranges of reading interests and abilities and perceptions. *Are You There, God? It's Me, Margaret* challenges and entertains eleven-year-old children to eighty-five-year-old adults. My university students re-read the book with an "Oh yes, isn't it funny; that was the way it was." The eleven-year-olds read the book with "I know exactly what Margaret is feeling." So, *Margaret* must be on my list of classics.

Blume's book has challenged and entertained readers from fourth grade to AARP. (I read it!) Margaret has a vague interest in whether she is Jewish or Christian. Her overshadowing interest is in knowing when she will become a "woman." She prays for her period because she doesn't want to be the last one of her friends to have one. She regularly does exercises to increase her 28" bust-size. Besides wanting to speed up her physical maturation, Margaret wants a meaningful relationship with God. Oh yes, she wants to know more about boys. Issues really haven't changed all that much, have they? I would suggest you not read this novel aloud. It is best experienced in the mind and heart of the reader. Because it is written in first person, the reader becomes Margaret.

Bosse, Malcolm J.
Cave Beyond Time
Thomas Y. Crowell, 1980.

Ben is a typical teenager who suffers the loss of his family in a car accident. He is resentful, deep in sorrow, and unable to understand why he must go to Arizona to live with his uncle. The uncle is an archaeologist on an archaeological dig in the American Southwest. "Why are these guys so interested in ancient handprints on the walls of a cave? So the hands are missing fingers." One morning, Ben wanders out across the desert, where he is bitten by several rattlesnakes. He wakes from a venom-induced trance to find himself displaced in time—not once, but three times. First, he lives with Stone Age nomads, then later with a tribe of bison hunters, and finally with the pueblo farmers. In each of the encounters with the past, he must accept the life as it is. These experiences of "beyond time" bring special meaning to Ben. When he is found and treated for his wounds, Ben is able to explain the mystery of the cave paintings. This is a gripping fantasy on the order of *A Wrinkle in Time* (L'Engle) and is great for reading aloud.

Cleary, Beverly
Ramona the Brave
William Morrow (Avon Camelot), 1975.
Illustrated by Alan Tiegreen.

Ramona will continue to be enjoyed by children of Ramona's age, as well as by older children who remember how it used to be. The adventures of

Ramona are family stories: a working mother, a father who loses his job and eventually returns to college, sisters' disagreements, and assorted other family crises. Each humorous story relates to problems which are small to grown-ups but loom very large in the lives of children. Ramona is her dramatic self in all situations. I remember wishing I could have been like Ramona when I first read Cleary as an adult. The entire family is worth modeling.

Collier, James and Christopher
My Brother Sam Is Dead
Four Winds Press, 1974.

Written in first person by Sam's younger brother Tim, this historical fiction is poignant in the telling of conflicting loyalties within a close family. The bitterness is never really crushed by the family. Sam is the only member of his Connecticut family to fight for the rebel cause. When he is falsely accused of stealing cattle from his own family, he is executed by his commanding officer as an example to others. Sam is a Loyalist. His family members are Tories. The sin of that difference is carried over to Sam. The outstanding section of the book is the epilogue written fifty years after Sam's death. I sometimes believe historical fiction is the best of books in retelling our historical past. That is certainly the case when the Colliers write.

Collier, James and Christopher
With Every Drop of Blood: A Novel of the Civil War
Laurel Leaf, 1996.

Fourteen-year-old Johnny joins up with a wagon train where he helps to bring food to the Southern armies. He is captured by a black soldier just about his age, and a deep friendship develops.

Curtis, Christopher Paul
Bud, Not Buddy
Delacorte, 1999.

Not too many books written for children use the Great Depression of the 1930s as the context. Out-of-work people, scarce food, and troubled times do not usually create suspense and excitement. In addition, what child can understand the impact of the stock market crash? These grim issues are more adult in nature. Yet Curtis creates the '30s setting and gives us Bud, a spunky protagonist of extraordinary strength, who is on a journey to find his dad, a jazz musician. Bud deals with death, homelessness, and racism along the way. Although he receives some help during his search, mainly Bud's own fortitude is celebrated. The resilience of the human spirit is awesome, and it is alive and well in Curtis' story.

Di Camillo, Kate
Because of Winn-Dixie
Candlewick Press, 2001.

"My name is India Opal Buloni, and last summer my daddy, the preacher, sent me to the store for a box of tomatoes and I came back with a dog." That is ten-year-old Opal talking. Can't you tell? The supermarket, of course, is Winn-Dixie. About the time Opal arrives for her groceries, a dog is running amuck in the store. When the red-faced, screaming store manager threatens to call the dog pound, Opal hollers, "Wait a minute!. . . That's my dog." Thus, Winn-Dixie becomes Opal's dog. After that, she and Winn-Dixie tell each other everything. Opal, lonely with no friends, having just moved to Florida, even tells Winn-Dixie about her mother, who left when Opal was three. The story creates levels of special meaning. On one level, it is the story about a child's love for a pet, a love that is as strong as one's love for a brother or sister. On another level, it is a story of making friends at church and at school because of this very special and unusual dog. *Because of Winn-Dixie* is so genuine, so hilarious, yet tender and melancholy, that it binds the heart of the reader/listener. This is a first novel for Di Camillo, and I hope not the last.

Fox, Paula
The Slave Dancer
Laurel Leaf, 1997.

Written with quiet understatements, Jessie, a white boy, accounts in first person his experiences of being kidnapped and forced to stay on board a slave ship. He is compelled to play his fife to exercise the slaves. These are not his worst moments. Jessie begins to see the slaves as fellow human beings, and he is transformed as he participates in acts of unforgettable brutality toward the slaves.

George, Jean
My Side of the Mountain
E. P. Dutton, 1959.

Children enjoy contemporary realism that rings with truth. Realistic fiction can be a window to the world, a world perhaps the reader has not experienced. Sam is a city boy who chooses to spend a winter alone on the land of his ancestors. The Catskills are foreboding and life-threatening. Sam has only read about surviving. He finds a hollow tree, makes a home, lays up food for the winter, sews buckskin clothing, and keeps a journal of the things he observes in his surroundings. This is a modern day "Robinson Crusoe." The author is a naturalist, which is certainly reflected in both the vivid details of the setting and the reader's sense of being there with Sam on his mountain.

Greene, Bette
Summer of My German Soldier
Bantam, 1973.

I have included *Summer of My German Soldier* just for me. Greene had not written her book when I was twelve years old, but I know the impact it would have had on me at that age. Girls of twelve and thirteen, those in-between years, need a "German soldier." It is a time for first infatuations; mine was Huckleberry Finn. This is a soft and gentle narrative coming out of a very stressful time for Patty Bergen, twelve years old and Jewish. She is "all legs," awkward, and shy. She lives with her mother and father in a small town in Arkansas. Her parents are cruel to her, as they exhibit no love for Patty. There is a German prisoner of war camp near town, and here she meets Anton, a handsome and knowledgeable young German prisoner. Patty thinks of Anton as her friend, so naturally she assists his escape. Anton escapes, but he is recaptured. Patty's role in his escape comes to light, and she is sent to reform school. Then Patty Bergen realizes that she will fulfill Anton's dream for her in the future. She will be a "person of value."

Grey, Zane
The Riders of the Purple Sage
Dover Publications, 2002.

The books by Zane Grey are often looked down upon as "not literature." Maybe not, but the action and characters truly reflect the American West. These books have caused many a young person to read and keep reading. The riders represent everything good, trustworthy, and stalwart in the American culture. The plot is rather pat, but who cares? The last days of the "old" west are exciting and longed for in the minds of the young and older alike.

Hinton, S. E.
The Outsiders
Puffin, 1997.

Problems of group identification are a part of all of S. E. Hinton's books especially *The Outsiders*, in which the greasers (i.e. the dirt heads) are in conflict with the socs (i.e. the society kids). The conflict in social classes proves to be the central focus of the youth in a typical high school. The setting is 1963. Could it be today? Certainly.

Howe, James and Deborah
Bunnicula
Antheneum, 1983.

Howe is one of the most personable authors writing for children today. He can not only write but can also talk to children about his books to inspire them to write their own. *Bunnicula* was written while Howe's wife Deborah, his co-author, was dying. He talks about this fact with children to show the strength of what writing can provide. In *Bunnicula*, the Monroe family returns from seeing the movie *Dracula* with a bunny they have found under the theater seat. The family pets, Chester the cat and Harold the dog, immediately recognize Bunnicula as a vampire. There are many clues the Monroes do not notice: the roaming of the bunny only at night; the red tomatoes and other vegetables drained of their juices and thus turned white, and the rabbit's moving in and out of his locked cage. The topper is a note, written in a Transylvanian dialect, found around the rabbit's neck. The story is told by Harold, the dog, and is filled with clever dog observations. The pun-filled tale is just pure fun.

Keene, Carolyn and Franklin W. Dixon
Nancy Drew Series; Hardy Boys Series
Grosset & Dunlap/Simon & Schuster.

These are formula series to be sure. But not always is formula a dirty word. Archetype has more positive connotations. The total predictability of both series is a fact. The heroine Nancy is strong, daring, and true to her mission—to unravel the mystery. The same is true of the boys of the Hardy Boys series. In the eras of the thirties and forties, these models were what was needed. The danger of the formula stories is that a reader will not be encouraged to read "deeper" novels.

Konigsburg, E. L.
From the Mixed-Up Files of Mrs. Basil E. Frankweiler
Atheneum, 1967.

Claudia is tired of the sameness of her life and its injustices. She has a dull existence. She wants to do something exciting and different, something more than setting the table and emptying the dishwasher on the same night that her little brother Jamie does nothing. Life is both boring and unfair. So Claudia decides to run away, and she chooses Jamie to run away with her because he has a bankroll of $24.43. Now where would you run if you were to run away from home? I don't think many children would choose to run to the Metropolitan Museum of Art, but that is what Claudia does. She and Jamie set up residence in the museum. They take baths in the museum's fountain and use the coins thrown into its pool as a source of income. The children eat at the automat and in the museum's cafeteria, and they continue their education by going on all of the museum's tours. While on one tour, Claudia becomes involved in a mystery related to the statue of a little angel, and while trying to solve the mystery, she meets Mrs. Basil E. Frankweiler. This is a story written within a story, and Konigsburg tells it with both sophistication and humor.

Lasky, Kathryn
Beyond the Divide
Laurel Leaf, 1986.

Meribah Simon is an Amish girl raised by strict rules. When she finds her father is going to be shunned by the Amish community and that he is leaving, she begs to go with him. Meribah and her father, Will, join the Gold rush wagon train for a fresh start. At their departure in St. Joseph, Missouri, Meribah is fascinated by the diversity of the emigrants. The emigrants share labor, food, and supplies along the trail, and spirits are high. As they travel through brutal terrain, an ominous change occurs. Her father becomes dangerously ill. The wagon train abandons them in the Sierra Nevada mountains. It is winter, and Will dies. Lasky creates a colorful group of nineteenth century personalities, in particular those who are Amish. The nearly surreal landscapes are vivid. Meribah is a luminous heroine with a spirit and will that are tested to the limits.

Lewis, C. S.
The Lion, the Witch and the Wardrobe
Macmillan, 1950.

The age-old conflict between right and wrong, good and evil, and life and death is seen over and over again in literature for children. The theme and the struggle are seen in cartoons (*Tom and Jerry*), folk tales (*Snow White*), modern fiction (*Sounder*), and fantasy. And fantasy brings me to C.S. Lewis. Lewis was a well-known scholar and theologian. He created a country called Narnia and wrote seven fantasies about the conflict between the children of Narnia and the wicked Snow Queen.

The Lion, the Witch and the Wardrobe, the first and the best in the series, begins quite realistically in "real" time as four children find their way into the land of Narnia through the back of a huge closet (wardrobe since it is British). The Snow Queen controls the weather so the land is covered with ice and snow—always winter and "never Christmas." The children and the Narnians challenge the evil witch and her associates: ghouls, hags, and boggles. Aslan the Lion comes with signs of spring. The children aid Aslan in destroying all that is evil in Narnia, and the lion crowns them Kings and Queens of Narnia.

Another in the series, *The Magician's Nephew*, is worth reading to older children. The beginnings of Narnia are developed in this second volume. These two books in the series are most appropriate for children. The stories are intriguing, enveloped in mystery, and wondrously adventurous. I am very cautious about the other five books. Lewis uses religious allegory throughout the Narnia stories. Young adults can appreciate and see the connections—most children see only the adventure. Is this fair to these beautifully written fantasies? Reserving the last five books in the series for the future may be the best plan. What's the rush?

Lowry, Lois
Number the Stars
Houghton Mifflin, 1989.

Lowry has written a simple, yet complicated story of Nazi persecution. Gory details of persecutions are not part of the moving experience of a Danish family and a Jewish family living in Denmark. The impact of the novel lies in its direct relationship with the "bridge-kid" reader. The Danish family saves the lives of their friends, the Rosens. The young daughters of each family are best friends. Annemarie and Ellen are initially and blissfully unaware of the danger in which they are living. The result of Nazi rule for Ellen is death; the result of Nazi rule for Annemarie is life. The horrors of this period of time are more poignantly expressed by Lowry than by any other author I know. And she does so with images which allow children to make connections: images of family, of friends, and of commitment.

Macaulay, David
Motel of the Mysteries
Houghton Mifflin, 1979.

I have probably given copies of *Motel of the Mysteries* as gifts to friends more often that I have given any other book, including adult books. The story is about us, as human beings. No matter how intellectual, how knowledgeable, how research-oriented—we humans can still get it wrong! In Macaulay's story, the year is 4044, and our hero, Howard Carson, is despondent. He has been working several years trying to produce a three-hump camel and has failed. He must get away. So he chooses to take a cruise to Usa, once the most advanced culture of the ancient world, destroyed by layers and layers of a substance called third-class mail during the twentieth century. In his despair, Howard wanders out onto the vast land of Usa. He falls into a deep pit, and when he recovers from the fall, he realizes he is looking at a sealed tomb. Elated, he starts digging, while thinking, "This may be the greatest discovery since that of the King Tut tomb in Egypt." In time, he gathers a team, equipment, and his trusted friend, Harriet Stone, and the dig begins in earnest.

So too has the fun of the reader/listener. In this case, what we, the readers, know about the tomb provides delight—for Carson's great discovery is nothing more than a simple motel. Macaulay writes, "Everything in the Outer Chamber (motel room) faced the Great Altar (television set), including the body of the deceased, which still lay on top of the Ceremonial Platform (bed)." He describes the items uncovered in the Inner Chamber (a bathroom): a Ceremonial Head Dress (shower cap), a highly polished white sarcophagus (bathtub), and a translucent curtain (shower curtain). The saga becomes more and more absurd with each description. And you cannot imagine the laughter of listeners as they exclaim, "We know. They don't!" This is a tale to be read aloud. The vocabulary is complex and scientific and can be difficult for even an excellent reader. The realistic charcoal drawings are a perfect match to the text.

Magorian, Michelle
Good Night, Mr. Tom
Harper & Row, 1981.

New perspectives are gained as a child has vicarious experiences through well-written literature. Good writing can transport the reader to other times and places. Identification with others allows the reader to enter a different world when he/she is tuned into the story. Magorian's powerful novel of an eight-year-old boy who is evacuated from London during World War II is unforgettable. And I do not use the term "unforgettable" lightly. Willie is sent to a small village in the English countryside. A terribly abused child of a deranged single mother, Willis is placed with a kindly but gruff widower who has become almost a recluse. Mr. Tom is suffering from the deaths of his wife and infant son.

Violence and sorrow are parts of the deeply moving story. Mr. Tom gains the faith, trust, and love of Willie by offering the deepest kind of love he can to a child who has never had that kind of devotion. Both Mr. Tom and Willie begin to heal, slowly and gently, from their former experiences. The village people, especially a village boy Jake, who is the same age as Willie, become so real you expect them to walk off the pages. The compassion and understanding everyone feels for Willie reaches a climax when Mr. Tom hears from Willie's mother wanting her son back. What can Mr. Tom do? I would highly recommend this book not be read aloud. It is for private thoughts, reflections, and dreams. You, though, must prepare the reader by reading it for yourself. After that, you will never be the same.

Maruki, Toshi
Hiroshima No Pika
HarperCollins, 1982.

This descriptive narrative looks at World War II, including the dropping of the atomic bomb from a Japanese perspective. This book is especially good to read aloud.

Milne, A. A.
Winnie the Pooh
E. P. Dutton, 1926. Illustrated by E. H. Shepard.

Don't confuse the television or movie versions of *Winnie the Pooh* with the real thing. Both television and movies change much in Milne's *Pooh* and corrupt the original concept of the delightful bear. Christopher Robin, patterned after Milne's son, has several favorite stuffed toys. Milne writes a separate adventure for each of them in *Winnie the Pooh*. What a fabulous gift to the world of children! The good friends include Pooh himself, a little bear of few brains; gloomy Eeyore, the donkey; Piglet, Pooh's best friend; and Tigger, a late-comer. Also there are Rabbit, Kanga, Roo, and Owl. They all live in the "100 Aker Wood," and they have all kinds of amusing adventures. My favorite adventure happens when Pooh gets into a very tight place and cannot get out. He decides that he cannot eat "hunny" until he grows thin enough to escape. The humor in the stories is not belly-laugh humor. Rather it is gentle and subtle. It creeps up on you. Many adults remember episodes from *Winnie the Pooh* and refer to them. My mother called my brother Christopher Robin. What did she call me? Tigger! Mother read a chapter at a time when our whole family was together on the brocade couch. We chuckled and laughed. Can you imagine knocking on your own door and wondering why no one is at home?

O'Dell, Scott
Sarah Bishop
Scholastic Paperbacks, 1991.

The story is based upon the life of Sarah Bishop who was born in England and came to the colonies shortly before the American Revolution. She and her family settled on Long Island. The most terrible night of her early life in the colonies was the raid by the Birdsalls who destroyed the family's Long Island farm. The Bishop family are Tories in a town of patriots. In a bitter aftermath of the raid, Sarah is alone. She retreats to the wilderness for refuge. There she begins to shape a new life.

Paterson, Katherine
Bridge to Terabithia
HarperCollins, 1977.

There are, in literature, models of ordinary boys and girls who find the courage to change and grow, to become loving persons, and to realize their own worth. Such is the beautifully written novel *Bridge to Terabithia*. Often on the lists of banned books, the story is about imaginary play. Jess Aarons, a ten-year-old artistic boy is a misfit to his family, and Leslie Burk, a new girl at her school, is considered a misfit by her peers. The two develop a friendship. These two lonely children invent a magical kingdom based upon Leslie's love for Narnia. They have their own Terabithia in the woods that can be reached only by swinging on a rope across a dry creek. One spring day, Leslie goes to Terabithia alone and drowns when the creek turns into a torrent. Jess is racked with grief. Through his sorrow, he comes to realize he has a more loving family than he had thought. To overcome his grief, he dwells on Leslie's gift to him: the ability to remember and imagine. This is a very emotional and subjective novel, and one of my favorites.

Rawls, Wilson
Where the Red Fern Grows
Macmillian, 1961.

No child should be denied the opportunity to hear *Where the Red Fern Grows* from the encirclement of an adult's arms. This heartwarming story is about love and devotion and tenacity. Billy lives in the Ozarks. He saves his hard-earned pennies to order two hound dogs. When Old Dan and Little Ann arrive, he trains them as a hunting team. One year, Billy enters his dogs in the annual coon hunt. Competing against twenty-five other teams of hounds, Old Dan and Little Ann endure a grueling five-day hunt, in which they nearly freeze to death during an unexpected blizzard that causes them to get lost. Despite everything, they win the cup. When Billy's family decides to move to Oklahoma, he chooses to remain with his grandfather and his beloved dogs. But then, a tragedy occurs. Old Dan is killed defending Billy against a mountain lion attack. Little Ann dies from pining for Old Dan. Where Billy buries his precious dogs, he finds a legendary red fern growing on the gravesite. The story is sentimental and memorable. I think of the devotion of Billy to his hound dogs as a part of what makes us human. I asked my mother when Cuddles died—I was five years old—if there were dogs in heaven. She replied, "Heaven is a place of love and joy, and since dogs are a part of joy, surely Cuddles will be there." What a satisfying concept!

Sachar, Louis
Holes
Farrar, Straus and Giroux, 1998.

What a talent to combine seriousness and humor in a single novel! This is the talent of Sachar. Stanley Yelnats is sent to a boys' juvenile detention center for a crime he did not commit, stealing a pair of sneakers. The detention center is in the heart of arid, hot Texas. As punishment, he is forced to dig holes in the desert with his fellow prisoners; for what reason, Stanley does not know. While digging, he makes friends and enemies among both fellow inmates and guards. When Stanley uncovers the mystery of Camp Green Lake, the lives of all those at the detention center change. In trying to solve the mystery, he also discovers why generations of his family have been unlucky. The characterizations are outstanding in their development. The plot is as complex as any scene in children's literature with the dark humor Sachar uses. This may be the first experience that "bridge-kids" have with this form of prose. Be aware of language if the book is read aloud.

Selden, George
The Cricket in Times Square
Farrar, Straus and Giroux, 1960.
Illustrated by Garth Williams.

An urban story where animals do most of the talking is rather rare. Selden gives this protagonist role to a fast-talking mouse named Tucker, who lives in Times Square with his pal, Harry, a cat. They meet a small country cricket named Chester, who spends a summer in Times Square with his pals. He arrives in Times Square in a picnic basket carried by a commuter from Connecticut. Tucker and Harry discover that Chester possesses a marvelous talent—he chirps musically! When Chester begins to give nightly concerts from the newsstand of his human friends, the Bellinis, he saves the family from bankruptcy as the crowds that gather to hear Chester chirp buy magazines and newspapers. Chester becomes so popular he brings traffic in New York City to a stop when he begins to sing opera.

This is a sweet, comforting story told in a peaceful manner. The art of Garth Williams gives appeal to the animals so they stand out as real personalities. This is a wonderful read-aloud story. I had a child ask me—I was reading sections of the story to a classroom of children in October 2001—if I thought Tucker and Harry were killed on September 11. Can you imagine the impact *A Cricket in Times Square* had made on that child? My response was very difficult to make. I explained that I thought Tucker and Harry were probably in Connecticut visiting Chester. I hope that was an appropriate answer.

Speare, Elizabeth
The Sign of the Beaver
Houghton Mifflin, 1983.

During the late sixteenth century, colonists pushed farther and farther into the wilderness of America. Many of my favorite stories have been set within this background. The search for a homestead, the fight to survive, and the strength of the pioneer spirit are the themes revealed in these stories. Speare's book is the story of Matt, a fourteen-year-old left to tend the new cabin he and his father built in Maine territory. The father tells Matt to take care of the homestead while he returns to Massachusetts for Matt's mother, younger brother, and the baby born while Matt and his father prepared the family cabin. Fourteen years old, can you imagine? Father tells Matt that he will be gone for about three months. During that time, things do not always go well for Matt: A trapper steals the only gun and takes all the sugar and flour and most of the supplies. Matt goes to a hollow honeybee tree to rob the bees of their honey and is severely stung. The grandson of the Chief of the Beaver Clan, Attean, rescues Matt and takes him to his grandfather. The story is wonderfully multi-themed without being didactic. Friendship, responsibility, courage, changing attitudes, and the need to understand a culture different from the one you know are present throughout the story. A perfect read-aloud book.

Taylor, Mildred
Roll of Thunder, Hear My Cry
Puffin, 1997.

A novel with the setting of the Great Depression, the narrative deals with the recent shameful past of poverty, racism, and terrorism. Cassie Logan is a spirited independent girl from a loving family and is the protagonist. In this one eventful year for the family, the violent climax is deeply felt by the reader.

Twain, Mark
The Adventures of Huckleberry Finn
(Various modern editions.) Scott, Foresman and Company, 1951 ed.

What is the appeal of books such as *Huckleberry Finn* for contemporary children? They are well-written stories with adventure and suspense. Their characterizations are magnificent, and the reading is enjoyable. My very first infatuation was with Huck. Oh, how I wished I could be Becky and join in on the escapades with Huck! Twain (Samuel Clemens) combines realism, humor, and an exciting adventure about growing up in a small town in mid-America in the nineteenth century. There is conflict between Twain's well-matched protagonist and antagonist—Huck versus Injun Joe. The plot is easy to comprehend, and you know Huck as a true hero who will win out, with some sacrifice on Huck's part. The unbelievable odds, the awesome danger, and the daring escapes all add to the thrill of the quest and chase. Reading aloud and retaining the American English vernacular of the nineteenth century adds to the feeling of how acceptable language can change. This is an important concept not to be neglected. Don't let this opportunity escape you.

White, E. B.
Charlotte's Web
Harper & Row, 1952. Illustrated by Garth Williams.

"Where is Pa going with that ax?" asked Fern of her mother. "A litter of pigs were born last night and he has to kill the runt." "Would Pa kill me if I were a runt?" Fern asks. Ever since I first read those lines in *Charlotte's Web*, the book has had a special spot for me. You see, some would consider my very small frame as runt-like. Unquestionably, White's novel is the most beloved story of the twentieth century. The true heroine of the story is a beautiful, large, gray spider who takes a little pig—the runt—and saves him. White develops many barnyard animals in the novel, but none are developed as fully as Charlotte and Wilbur.

Charlotte, the spider, promises to save Wilbur from the butcher, and she does. She guides Wilbur to becoming a confident pig with the messages she spins in her web: "Some pig! Terrific! Radiant! Humble!" But, while Wilbur is saved, Charlotte dies. And so, Wilbur, in a tender effort to repay Charlotte and to continue her legacy, brings Charlotte's egg sac back to the farm to protect from harm's way. I must not forget Templeton—a true antagonist! The story—for me—is about friendship. No one should try to name all the themes. Children will decide for themselves. White did not originally write this story for children, but children have taken it for their own. The humor, the pathos, the in-depth character development, the tenderness, and the determination are all elements revealed in the sensory language of both the narrative and the conversations. The pen-and-ink drawings of Garth Williams are adorable. (What a word to use concerning art!) This is one of two books of fiction at the top of *Clodfelter Classics*.

Wilder, Laura Ingalls
Little House on the Prairie
HarperCollins, 1953. Illustrated by Garth Williams.

The wilderness of the exploration era of America coupled with the pioneer spirit of the settlers who faced its challenge provide exciting plots and settings for a number of children's stories. One such set of stories is Laura Ingalls Wilder's Little House series. The series is a saga describing the growing up of the Ingalls family. In the first book, *Little House in the Big Woods*, Laura is six years old, and in the last book, *The First Four Years*, Laura is married to Manley and teaching. The stories are based on Wilder's life in the 1870s and 1880s. The difficulties and joys of the pioneer family are described.

Charlotte Huck, in *Children's Literature in the Elementary School*, offers a beautiful metaphor relating to these books. She writes, "Throughout the stories the warmth and security of family love runs like a golden thread that binds the books to the hearts of their readers." The childlike fun of Laura in the first book reflects the pioneer child. After Pa does his butchering, Laura plays with the pig's bladder as she watches it swirl down the creek. As Laura matures, so do her activities. Her love for her sister, Mary, stricken by illness that causes her to lose her sight, is especially touching. There are grasshopper plagues, marauding bears, Indians, blizzards, floods, and near starvation. There are the joyous Christmas seasons, real glass for windows, trips to town, and Pa's fiddling during long winter nights. Moving from Wisconsin to Minnesota to Kansas to Dakota Territory is experienced with the security of family always in place. I cannot neglect mentioning Garth Williams' meaningful pen-and-ink drawings. He creates the images of the Ingalls family as they surely must have been.

Information Books

(and Biographies)

Curtis, Patricia
Cindy: A Hearing Ear Dog
Penguin Putnam Books for Young Readers, 1981.

Most children have a great love and empathy for dogs. Often the death of a pet is devastating for a child. This book deals with an abandoned dog that becomes not only a beloved pet but also a companion for a deaf girl. Cindy is picked up wandering the streets by the dog pound. From there, she is taken to a hearing dog center where she is trained as a hearing-ear dog. The stages of the training are realistically and beautifully told through both text and photographs. How a hearing-ear dog aids in being the ears of her mistress is remarkable. Most children know about seeing-eye dogs. Now, they can learn about another way that pets can assist a human being.

d'Aulaire, Ingri and Edgar Parin d'Aulaire
Abraham Lincoln
Doubleday & Company, 1939.

Children probably recognize the art (lithographs) of the d'Aulaires on sight. The oversized books with somewhat idealized pictures enhance their stories tremendously. Written primarily for an audience not yet reading, the d'Aulaires know their audience. They know the intrigue children have with the childhood of famous people, so the authors/illustrators have stressed the childhood of Abraham Lincoln, Christopher Columbus, and George Washington in their biographies. Their biography of Abraham Lincoln is my favorite. The style is fictionalized biography. The most-known events in Lincoln's childhood are dramatized in the illustrations and text. While the d'Aulaires have been criticized for not creating a birth-to-death biography, they are not concerned. In response to the critics, they say, "We want children to remember the greatness of the man, not how he died." Good reasoning!

Freedman, Russell
Children of the Wild West
Clarion Books, 1983.
Illustrated by George Buctel.

Freedman uses photographs to extend his biography in a stunning manner. This biography is critical, in that it documents the details of the everyday lives of children from the many cultures who were in the Wild West during the 1840–1860 period. Indian children, immigrant children, and Chinese children are included. The photographs are from archival sources when cameras were scarce. Photos of covered wagons, log cabins, sod houses, and schoolrooms show real children with their modes of dress and meager possessions. Indian children "before and after" are especially poignant—first, in their tribal dress and, later, in their Americanized clothes after being sent to government boarding schools. This is an astounding photobiography of images and narratives that linger in the mind long after the book is closed.

Freedman, Russell
Give Me Liberty! The Story of the Declaration of Independence
Holiday House, Inc., 2000.

"All men are created equal," Jefferson wrote. "They have certain God-given rights, including the rights to Life, Liberty and the pursuit of Happiness. Governments are created to secure those rights." Today the Declaration of Independence is an eloquent treatise on human liberty. At the time of its creation, it was a dangerous political statement involving profound personal risks to its signers and supporters. During two weeks, Thomas Jefferson drafted and redrafted the Declaration. The Continental Congress made some changes, and the document emerged. The Declaration is a timeless affirmation of human rights and representative government. The magnificent oil paintings in the book are familiar to all. Well-written and quick paced, this is a biography that reads as a novel.

Freedman, Russell
The Life and Death of Crazy Horse
Holiday House, Inc., 1996.

Careful biographies find a balance between telling too much and telling enough to portray a person's life as accurately as they can. Freedman's biography of Crazy Horse is an outstanding example of this balance. He never moves beyond documentation despite the fact that there is little accurate information about this Indian warrior and leader. In telling the story, Freedman depends primarily on personal interviews conducted with Crazy Horse's comrades fifty years ago. Curly (Crazy Horse) was light-skinned with curly, brown hair. He was stout and short of stature. He never bragged, never took a coupe count, and never scalped his enemies. He was thought to be "with spirit" and could not be injured by arrow or bullet. These pieces of information were documented in interviews fifty years after the Battle of the Little Bighorn. This is fictionalized biography at its very best, and it is typical of the work of Russell Freedman.

Fritz, Jean
Traitor: The Case of Benedict Arnold
Putnam Juvenile, 1981.

When Benedict Arnold was a young man, some people in his home-town of Norwich, Connecticut, predicted that he'd grow up to be a success. Others said he would turn out badly. As it happened, everyone was correct. Benedict Arnold succeeded beyond anyone's wildest expectations. George Washington in 1777 called him "the bravest of the brave." Yet three years later, he was described as "the villain of villains past," and no one would have argued with that. Fritz writes history like an adventure, like a detective story. The book is well researched, and the motives of America's most famous traitor are well developed.

Fritz, Jean
Where Do You Think You're Going, Christopher Columbus?
G. P. Putnam's Sons, 1980. Illustrated by Margot Tomes.

This biography is for young children. While written in an authentic biography style, this book is appealing to children because of the talent of Fritz. He creates biography that is entertaining, fast moving, and humorous. These three ingredients are found in all of Fritz's biographies. Documented evidence is so woven into the text that it seems as if Fritz is just talking about Columbus as a good friend. The sensitive and revealing artwork of Tomes clarifies and deepens the story.

Jakes, John
Susanna of the Alamo: A True Story
Voyager Books, 1990. Designed and illustrated by Paul Bacon.

"Remember the Alamo!" resonates through history—a cry that evokes memories of Davy Crockett, Jim Bowie, and William Barrett Travis—three of the many heroes who died there. Do you remember Susanna Dickinson? Probably not. She survived the massacre to tell its story. Were it not for Mrs. Dickinson, the Alamo might have been forgotten. She was spared death by Mexico's General Santa Anna so that she could bear witness of his might to Sam Houston's rebel Texas army. Susanna scorned the General's attempt to make her his emissary. Her chilling story has never been written so vividly for young people. The masterful illustrations are deeply moving. Use as a read-aloud for young adults.

Lawson, Robert
Ben and Me
Little, Brown and Company, 1939.

Biographies are stories of people's lives and, like all stories, are dependent on the author. Accuracy, portrayal of the subject, and style are hallmarks of good writing. All styles are interpretation, and all biography styles are based on recognized forms of documentation. There are qualities of style for children's literature, and when recommending a book to a child or selecting a book to read to a child, an adult must carefully consider style. An appealing style invites the child to read other biographies. An unappealing style discourages the child from reading them. As parents and teachers, we often "kill" the choosing of biographies because we do not understand the importance of style.

There are three styles for biography: clinical, where even the dialogue is based on some record of what was actually said by particular people; fictionalized biography, which includes reconstructed events and conversations; and biographical fiction that is natural and "fun" to read. *Ben and Me* is a hilarious story about Benjamin Franklin, narrated by his mouse, Amos, who lives in Ben's fur hat. All facts are correct except, of course, Amos's insistence that he had invented all those things (pot belly stove), discovered those things (lightning is electricity), and started those things (public hospitals) for which Ben Franklin is usually given credit. The illustrations are rather ill-matched with the text, but that doesn't seem to matter. This is a wonderful book to read aloud, especially if early American history is the topic. I read *Ben and Me* to eighth-grade students, and they loved it.

McKissack, Patricia and Fredrick
Sojourner Truth: Ain't I a Woman?
Scholastic, 1992.

In 1797, a slave named Isabella was born in New York State. She was freed in 1827, but it was not until later that she chose the name by which she would become known throughout the nation and remembered long after her death. The name she chose was "Sojourner Truth." She was the mother of five children. One of her sons was sold illegally to a southerner. She brought suit against that white man and won. Sojourner was a preacher, an abolitionist, and an activist for the rights of both blacks and women. Sojourner could not read, but she could quote the Bible word for word. She was six feet tall with a profound faith in God's love. This is an inspirational biography of an African-American woman who fought for freedom.

McNeer, May
America's Abraham Lincoln
Houghton Mifflin, 1997. Illustrated by Lynd Ward.

To those who knew him, he was "sad, and funny—kind, and thoughtful—ugly, and somehow noble." Abraham Lincoln embodied the spirit of freedom and the democratic ideals which he upheld and preserved as a heritage for all peoples. McNeer's biography of Lincoln is a discerning one, written with remarkable clarity, telling of his growth in spiritual strength, wisdom, and understanding throughout his whole life. The full color, vivid illustrations and the black and white half-tone drawings of Ward portray the stature of the boy and the man who was the sixteenth president of the United States.

Meltzer, Milton
Columbus and the World Around Him
Franklin Watts, 1990.

This is a carefully researched and written narrative describing the other events during the time of Columbus and his trips to the New World. Many of the controversies over his arrival in the Americas are developed.

Note: Meltzer is recognized as one of the finest writers in the genre of historical novels. Some of his other titles include *Brother Can You Spare a Dime?; The Hispanic Americans; The Black American: A History in Their Own Words, 1619–1983, Voices from the Civil War; Thomas Jefferson: The Revolutionary Aristocrat; Frederick Douglass: In His Own Words; and Langston Hughes: An Illustrated Edition.* (There are several other titles written by Meitzer.)

Meyer, Carolyn
Where the Broken Heart Still Beats: The Story of Cynthia Ann Parker
Gulliver Books, 1992.

In May of 1836, nine-year-old Cynthia Ann Parker was kidnapped from her home in West Texas by a raiding band of Comanche warriors. Twenty-five years later, Naduah (Cynthia Ann) was a Comanche. She was the wife of a chief and the mother of a baby girl and two young warriors. She was ignorant of her past as a pioneer girl. Then suddenly Naduah and her baby were recaptured by Texas Rangers and returned to her former homestead. Against her will, she was forced to conform to a new life among white people. Naduah struggled to understand these settlers' ways and to remember a language she no longer spoke. Her hope came from the fact that her feared son, Quanah, would find her and return her to her people, the Comanche. In this outstanding novel, Meyer creates a first person diary written by Cynthia Ann's cousin Lucy Parker. The narrative is a moving account of the tragic life of a young girl who is caught between the Comanche and the settlers.

Mills, Judie
John F. Kennedy
Franklin Watts, 1988.

Fifty-four years after his assassination, historians are tentatively evaluating John F. Kennedy's achievements and reassessing his role in shaping American policy. Although his legacy is still uncertain, the spell he cast over the minds of whole generations has left an indelible mark. Mills has written a biography of a very complicated man and his family with feelings of a contemporary—she was there. Kennedy came from a deeply religious family on his mother's side. His father was a hard driving, self-made millionaire with an obsession for a son of his to be president of the United States. Through a series of accidents, John fulfilled his father's dream. The narratives of the childhood and youth of Kennedy are especially moving.

O'Dell, Scott
Streams to the River, River to the Sea
Fawcett, 1987.

This is a brilliant novel—Scott O'Dell's last one. The reader is presented the travels of Merriweather Lewis and William Clark through the eyes of Sacagawea (sak-a-ja-way-ah). Thomas Jefferson was a genius president with far-reaching ideas. He knew this young country of the United States was surrounded by enemies and false friends: France, Spain, and England. At last, he comes up with a wonderful idea. He would ask Congress to buy Louisiana from the French. Meanwhile, so as not to arouse suspicion, he would gather a band of young men to explore the northeast, a wilderness that no white man had ever seen. France agreed to the sale for fifteen million dollars, a paltry amount because Louisiana was bigger than the whole United States. Lewis (29) and Clark (33) were chosen. Sacagawea was a Shoshone, a tribe who lived high in the Rocky Mountains. She went to guide Lewis and Clark on foot, on horseback, and by canoe, four thousand miles on a journey that ranks in courage and danger with any journey of recorded history. (I wish I had been with them!)

Patterson, Lillie
Martin Luther King, Jr. and the Freedom Movement
Checkmark Books, 1997.

Few freedom fighters have had as great an impact on the world as Martin Luther King, Jr. His story of the nonviolent struggle to achieve his "dream" is the subject of this well chronicled narrative. The significant events—the Montgomery bus boycott, the sit-ins, the marches and protests—are developed in vivid details.

St. George, Judith
So You Want to Be President?
Philomel Books, 2000. Illustrated by David Small.

St. George reveals special talent in combining little known facts and humor in *So You Want to Be President?* Small's appropriate cartoon-style illustrations perfectly match the clever and witty text. The humorous tidbits about the president's office seem to create a great deal of discussion. Children love to add to the information. "My daddy says presidents must be married," said one child when I was reading the story to him and his classmates. "A person who becomes president must play golf," added another. The interest created by the book is tremendous. Make hay!

Stephens, Ann S.
Malaeska: The Indian Wife of the White Hunter
The John Day Co., 1929.

This is the story of a hunter and his Indian wife in the Revolutionary days in upper New York. This may be rather melodramatic, but its emphasis is more on thrills and chills than tears.

Yates, Elizabeth
Amos Fortune, Free Man
E. P. Dutton & Company, Inc., 1950.

Complete biography spans its subject's lifetime—from birth to death. This is the case with *Amos Fortune, Free Man*. The subject of the story is a little-known black man. The moving account of a man born free in Africa, sold as a slave in North America, and later purchases his own freedom and the freedom of other slaves, is inspiring. Details surrounding Amos's purchase of Violet, a young black woman, and the love that develops between them is the most striking section of the biography. Amos and Violet marry and live as devoted husband and wife for over fifty years. Their tombstones and the inscriptions on them were pictured on the final pages. An awesome ending!

Traditional Literature

Andersen, Hans Christian
The Ugly Duckling
Morrow Junior Books, 1999.
Adapted and illustrated by Jerry Pinkney.

Andersen is generally thought of as being the first author of modern fairy tales, although his stories have many of the same archetypal elements as folktales. The literary fairy tale utilizes the form of folktales with an identifiable author. The Grimms collected the tales of folk; they did not write them. I use care when reading Andersen's fairy tales to young children. His fairy tales are often cruel, morbid, and obsessed with death. *The Steadfast Tin Soldier* and *The Little Match Girl* leave a sense of helplessness in the listener. *The Ugly Duckling* is my favorite, although *The Princess and the Pea* runs a close second. Just be careful with Andersen's fairy tales with children below the age of nine. Andersen thought of *The Ugly Duckling* as his autobiography. The marvelously fanciful images produced by Pinkney are magnificent and sensory. He adapted the fairy tale from original sources, so the pain, compassion, and triumphs of the duckling can be "felt" by the listener. The narrative is written into the double-page spreads of glorious watercolors. From the oddly shaped sixth egg to the raising of a swan's slender neck in pure joy, the tale has beauty and grace.

Bowden, Joan Chase
Why the Tides Ebb and Flow
Houghton Mifflin, 1979. Illustrated by Marc Brown.

A pourquoi tale (from the French word for "why") seeks to explain a natural phenomenon. Examples are *Why the Sea Is Salty, Why a Jack Rabbit's Ears Are Long, Why the Sky Is Blue*. Every family has its own pourquoi tales. My mother walked with her toes turned out. I asked her why she walked so fancy, lady-like. She responded with a wonderful pourquoi tale of the Clodfelter family. Ask me about it. I asked my father once why his legs were so short, and he said, "My legs are just long enough to reach the ground!" I thought this was so brilliant! Years later, I read that Abraham Lincoln had said the same thing!

Why the Tides Ebb and Flow is a West African folktale and, as such, has some special characteristics. African tales most often have what I call double or triple pourquois or "whammies." In this story, there is an old woman who wants a hut. She goes to the Great Sky Spirit and asks him to give her a rock so she can build her hut, but the Great Sky Spirit is too busy and tells her to come back. She goes back again and again, until finally the Great Sky Spirit grows tired of her nagging and tells her to take one—any rock she wants. The old woman knows exactly the rock she wants. She gets into her stewpot and sails and sails out into the sea. "Listen to me, old woman, you are getting too close to the rock in the hole in the sea," the birds, the fish, and finally the Great Sky Spirit say to her. "Then I am going in the right direction," she replies. Well, sure enough, she takes the rock from the hole in the sea, and that is the beginning of the pourquois. You must read the tale aloud and especially dwell on the three pourquois at the end. Priceless! While discussing this story, have the children add their own pourquoi stories, ones that come from their families.

Bryan, Ashley
The Night Has Ears: African Proverbs
Atheneum Books, 1999.

"A man with a cough cannot conceal himself." –Yoruba

"Treat your guest as a guest for two days; on the third day, give him a hoe." –Swahili

We all have proverbs for any and every situation. When my mother would ask me or my brother to do something and we would ask "Why?" she would say, "If you have a barking dog, why bark yourself?" Think of the proverbs you use: "well begun is half-done; don't count your chickens before they hatch; practice makes perfect; and Rome wasn't built in a day." Proverbs teach, they provide humor, and they are fun to say. They abound in the oral tradition and in the written literatures of all people. These African proverbs have inspired stories, which give them meaning. They also give insights into the culture and customs of the people that developed them. This is a good book with bold, vivid illustrations that say to the reader, "have fun!"

d'Aulaire, Ingri and Edgar Parin d'Aulaire
D'Aulaire's Book of Greek Myths
Doubleday & Co., Inc., 1962.

The most familiar myths to Americans are the Greek myths. There are many anthologies consisting of the stories of gods and goddesses, heroes, and monsters. They deal with mortals and their relationships to gods who look, and sometimes act, like mortal men. My personal favorite Greek myths are the tales of Perseus, Pegasus, Medusa, Andromeda, and Cassiopeia. The d'Aulaires have written and illustrated a "complete biography" of the Greek gods. The vivid colors create the mood of the ancient Greeks. The design is outstanding in keeping with the myths. There is no slang to distract from the magnificent tales. The style is very readable, even if there is no pronunciation guide. If younger children are required to read the book, it will destroy any love for the myths. It is a wonderful book to read aloud slowly and at one's leisure.

Grimm, Jakob and Wilhelm
Grimm's Household Stories
Mayflower Books, Inc., 1979. Translated by Lucy Crane.

When Jakob and Wilhelm Grimm published the first volume of *Household Stories* in 1812, they did not intend it for children. They were linguists and were studying the language and grammar of the "language of the folks." Then how did folk literature become associated with children? The pure entertainment and the kindling of the imagination charm them. Born of the oral tradition, the tales are best when "told." Dreams can come true! This collection of nearly seventy-five stories carefully preserves the form and content of the tales. These tales come directly out of the translation from the German language to English. The conflicts between good and evil, the kind and the sinister, and the beautiful and the ugly are carefully preserved.

While Walt Disney may be credited with popularizing the Grimm tales, he is also responsible for corrupting the tales to the point that the Grimms would not have recognized them. Disney turned the tales into melodramas for the sake of his movies. The dwarfs are now cute little men with names. Snow White is a sweet teenager who dances before she eats but, in the original tale, is just seven years old when she is banished to the forest to be killed. These tales are a rightful part of a child's literary heritage and lay the groundwork for understanding all literature. Charlotte Huck says, "As you meet recurring patterns or symbols in myths like floods, savior heroes, cruel stepmothers, the seasonal cycle of the year, the cycle of a human life, you begin to build a framework for literature." The Crane collection uses full-page black block prints. The art is certainly not the charm of the comprehensive Grimm stories. Read aloud, read aloud, read aloud.

Jarrell, Randall
Tales from the Brothers Grimm: Snow White and the Seven Dwarfs
Farrar, Straus, and Giroux, 1972. Retold from Jakob and Wilhelm Grimm. Illustrated by Nancy Elholm Burkert.

In this beautiful edition of *Snow White*, retold by Randall Jarrell, Burkert's illustrations challenge Walt Disney's sappy interpretation. Burkert has obviously researched the German Snow White and has drawn no funny dwarfs, but dwarfs of grotesque dimensions. After all, the dwarfs in the Grimm's tales hide in the forest because of their gruesome appearance. Snow White is drawn as a real child, not as a glamorous woman. The medieval cottage of the dwarfs is authentic from those times, the plates and mugs are copied from museum pieces, and Snow White wears appropriate clothing for a young girl. All the items pictured in Burkert's illustrations symbolize innocence, love, kindness, and protection against evils. Jarrell is true to Grimm's story. Shaking the apple free from her mouth awakened Snow White, not the kiss of the prince in Disney's version. And the climax is as the Grimms collected it: The jealous queen has to put on the red-hot iron slippers and dance until she dies. Most adults do not care for Jarrell's and Burkert's *Snow White*. That is such a shame, for this book has restored the beauty, symbolism, and dignity of the tale.

Lester, Julius
The Tales of Uncle Remus (Four Volumes)
Dial Books, 1987. Illustrated by Barry Moser.

Anyone who tries to read the original Uncle Remus Tales, collected by Joel Chandler, unless the dialect has been simplified, finds the tales almost impossible to read and tell and even more difficult to understand. Now come the tales written in the authentic speech patterns of the legendary South, the American rural south—they are presented by Lester as gifts to all. The animals speak in the dialect of the people "I'z bon and bread in de briar patch. Hippity, hippity." (The text is written primarily in Standard English that makes the reading so much easier.) The trickster, the protagonist, and the antagonist are one: Bruh Rabbit. He leads the way to all kinds of mischief. (Every culture has a Bruh Rabbit. In the Plains Indian culture, he is Kokopelli, the sly, trick-playing mastermind.) The other characters—Bruh Bear, Bruh Possum, Bruh Fox—all play their special and constant roles as the fun rises and ebbs with their shenanigans. The Moser paintings are enchanting with vivid colors, and the "crude" art style he uses is perfect. The full-page and double-page spreads intensify the tales. Don't read too many tales at once—space them out.

Prelutsky, Jack, selector
The Random House Book of Poetry for Children
Random House, 1983. Illustrated by Arnold Lobel.

Poetry is often destroyed in our schools today by the very people who should be promoting the beauty of poetry. How is this done? Through forced memorization of poetry, using poetry with no context or meaning for the child, and the forced writing of a "poem" before lunch—"so get busy; you have already wasted five minutes." One cannot create in a vacuum! Poetry is high-frequency language; it has intensity and no wasted words. Prose is just the opposite: it wastes words and it is lackadaisical. Be very careful that you do not add to this destruction. Jack Prelutsky has written some of the most light-hearted and humorous verse for children. He plays with language, and at the same time, his poems show a caustic wit appealing to children. *The Random House Book of Poetry* is perfect for the classroom and the home. There are over five hundred poems, thirty-nine by Prelutsky himself. The best-known poets are represented in the collection. Lobel has profusely illustrated the collection with pictures on each and every page. This is a wonderful anthology that will draw children to it.

Silverstein, Shel
Where the Sidewalk Ends
Harper & Row, 1974.

This collection of humorous poetry written and illustrated by Silverstein was on best-seller lists for many months. Read by both children and adults, it is probably the best known among teachers. Silverstein's weird and unusual combination of words fascinates the readers. The strange sounding words, the coined words, the amusing situations, and the slightly unsavory drawings pull the readers into the poems. The crocodile who is a dentist, Rosy who eats her toes, the boy who is a television set, and the king who eats only peanut butter—all create a zany and memorable collection. The poems appeal to the primitive sense of humor in us all yet should not be used in a steady diet of poetry.

Williams, Jay
Everyone Knows What a Dragon Looks Like
Four Winds Press, 1976. Illustrated by Mercer Mayer.

Do you know what a dragon looks like? Can you describe one? Well, it has scales, is green, blows fire and smoke and . . . Oh no, I see you don't know what a dragon looks like. Mayer's illustrations are done in Oriental style to capture the spirit of Williams' modern fairy tale. Han is the poor little gate sweeper for the city of Wo in China. He is the first one to see the dragon. "Good morning, kind sir," Han says to the little, old, bald, fat man as he enters the city gates. "The city is praying for the dragon to come and save us from destruction at the hands of the horsemen from the North. The Mandarin and his counselors have been praying for the great dragon to come and protect Wo." "I know," says the little man. "I am a dragon!" So, you see, looks can be deceiving! Mayer's art, with its heavy oils and borders of Oriental figures, is magnificent. The double-page spreads allow the dragon to extend over the pages so the grandeur of the scenes is heightened. The humor exhibited by children when the tale is read is pure joy. Of course, they all know what a dragon looks like down to the most minute detail. And of course, they roll with laughter when the little, old, bald, fat man is a dragon. You hear, "Read it again!" This is a tongue-in-cheek fairy tale with spirit and vigor. Looks can be deceiving!

Wolkstein, Diane
White Wave
Thomas Y. Crowell, 1979. Illustrated by Ed Young.

I read and quote from this awesome retelling of *White Wave* more than from any other selection I have in this book. I read the tale as often to adults as to children. The original story has been lost "in the mist of time." It is Chinese in origin. Wolkstein's powerful text and Young's mysterious but grand illustrations create a unified image. A young Chinese farmer is in deep sorrow—his mother and father are dead, and he is too poor to marry. He stumbles on a shell one evening on his way home. He picks it up and discovers within it an earth snail that is alive. He puts the shell on the table and some food beside it. He comes home the next evening, and a delicious meal has been prepared for him. He looks and sees no one. Each evening, he finds freshly prepared food and often flowers on the table. His entire life changes. He goes to work eagerly, and he comes home eagerly. One day, he doubles back and sees a young woman rising from the shell. He rushes in, and she tells him she must now leave because "he forgot what he knew." She tells him, however, that if he is ever in great need to call her, White Wave, and she will come to him. As the story continues, he does need her, and he picks up the empty shell and calls her by name. Out of the shell pours the purest of rice. He gains new strength, marries, and has children. He tells them about White Wave. He builds a shrine in her honor.

In time, the man dies, and his family disappears. Eventually even the shrine disappears, and all that is left is the story. The young man's words are the climax to the tale: "Only the unwise think that which is dead is gone. The story goes on forever. And that is how it is with all of us—when we die, all that remains is the story." I often ask my students: what of your story will remain?

Fantasy, Science Fiction

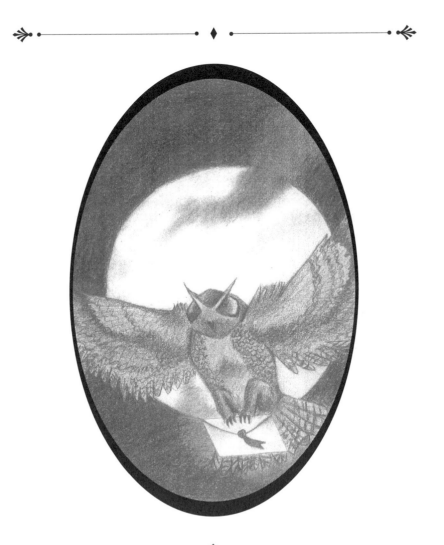

L'Engle, Madeleine
A Wrinkle in Time
Dell Publishing, 1962.

A Wrinkle in Time may be the classic science fiction for all children of the twentieth century. It is a multi-themed story that can be read on many levels. Charles Wallace Murry is five going on thirty. He is brilliant. He has a special relationship with his practical and stubborn sister, twelve-year-old Meg. Their father, a scientist working for the government, is missing. With the help of Calvin O'Keefe, a fourteen-year-old friend, and Mrs.Whatsit, Mrs. Who, and Mrs. Which, three little old women with magical powers, Meg and Charles Wallace travel to rescue Mr. Murry. How they travel captivates the reader, by means of a *tesseract*, a wrinkle in time. Mr. Murry is rescued, but Charles is left behind on the evil planet. Meg realizes that she is the only one who can bring her brother back to the family. Only Meg can defeat "It," the story's grotesque antagonist. With what does Meg defeat "It"? LOVE! *A Wrinkle in Time* is a complex novel. I have found that reading it aloud is best, after which most children choose to read it for themselves.

Rowling, J. K.
Harry Potter and the Chamber of Secrets
Scholastic Press, 1998.

I am appalled by the reaction of some adults in their "fear" of the Harry Potter books. The imagination is the soul of the human being. If we can't imagine, we can't hope, and if we can't hope, life isn't worth living. Rowling makes us a vast array of magic devices: the Quidditch broom of Harry's, the invisible cloaks, the owls that deliver mail—all so original. This is the fantasy world of Hogwarts, a school for bizarre and intriguing magic. There is logic to all the magic based upon Rowling's own creations. She never violates or goes beyond her own creation. To deny children the stories of Harry

Potter and his adventures is to deny children their childhood. Readers have devoured each book as it has been printed. Every generation and culture has its folkloric sprites, giants, elves, talking animals, and hobbits. Now we have the creatures of Rowling's fantasy world. What a gift she has given to the world of children and adults alike.

Epilogue

Afterthoughts

June, 2007

*W*ell, that's it. Ninety-six books I hold as classics at this moment in time. How many of these books will be on my list five, ten, or even twenty years from now, I cannot say. The only thing I really know for sure is there will be changes and additions because to stay alive, to be invigorated by one's work, there must be change. Change can also be called "learning."

I hope my list of books will stimulate teachers and parents to say, "Oh my, she didn't include *Dear Mr. Henshaw* (Cleary) or *The Snowy Day* (Keats). How could she have neglected *Sam, Bangs, and Moonshine* (Ness)? She should be ashamed!" Yet, these ninety-six are my classics. What are yours?

"I know well that only the rarest kind of best in anything can be good enough for the young!"[1] This often-quoted statement by Walter de la Mare is true, but "the best" is not what my list is about. Thus, my choices are not "the best" if one's measuring stick is "good" literature. Instead, my list is personal, growing out of my own beginnings in a "reading" family and continuing through my years teaching young and not-so-young students all the way to my present work on a university level with those who will lead their own students in the future. While Nancy Drew and Cherry Ames may not make a list of "best" in children's literature, they remain on my list as two of my favorites. Their characters may be flat in development, but Nancy and Cherry were and are important in my own continuing story.

Ken Goodman, the noted linguist and my teacher, explains that reading frees the minds and creative energies in children for the greatest gain of the whole child. Once the enjoyment of reading takes over a child, young adult, or an adult, the affective domain—the need or desire to read "a good book"—cannot be thwarted. It is addictive! "Where did you learn to read, Granddaddy?" asks the young child as his granddad is reading to him. "Sitting at the feet of desire is the only place anyone learns anything," replies the old man. I believe the truth in that statement, that desire is provoked as probably all learning is provoked. The desire to read comes usually from another human being, and there lies the great responsibility of parents and teachers: to stimulate, to provoke the child's desire to read.

Each time I write about children and their literature, I immerse myself in that literature and become thrilled and really astonished at how the books have evolved within me. Both the books written a century ago and those written just last year get better and better. How can this be, I ask myself. How can a book with the same number of pages, the same pictures, and the same text be better now than it was when I read it a year ago or ten years ago? With the "older books," those that I know so well that I can "tell them" rather than read them, their telling allows the words to connect to new images that sink deep into my soul, constructing anew who I am and who I am becoming. Thus, the retelling of familiar stories offers fertile ground for the imagination. With words so familiar that they come automatically to the lips, the mind is left free to imagine—to seek out new images with which to connect "old" words. In this way, each "old" word becomes a treasure chest into which more and more treasure is deposited. As I offer these treasures to my students, I pass on the images and the passions that are my life. In their telling, these old, familiar tales become my stories—my joy.

The "new" books, the first time read-to-self or read-to-others stories, allow for surprise, freshness, and curiosity. Their invitation for "toying with an idea and/or concept" is invigorating. Do I need to remember the exact words of the author? No, thank heavens. Instead, the essence of the story and the desire to read special parts again and again overwhelm me. With these "new" books, in spontaneous re-remembering the story comes alive for me.

As children hear and are led to discover good stories, their pleasure increases, and they begin to look for other good stories. Telling a child that he/she can read without creating a reading environment is a huge mistake. The child needs provoking—either from images created by a teacher or parent or from within a classroom, a home, or even the backseat of the car on the way to school. The opportunities to inculcate are always present. And the memories created during reading bring a multi-sensory expression to reading, for one reads with the smells, touches, tastes, and sounds of these moments. Each time I read or tell *Charlotte's Web*, I smell my mother's wonderful scent, and her smell takes the story deeper into my being. When I read or tell *The Little Engine That Could*, I hear Miss Williams, my third grade teacher, and the sounds she made just like the little engine. I hear Miss Williams, and I imitate her. Sir Francis Bacon wrote, "Some books are to be tasted, other to be swallowed, and some few to be chewed and digested."

These books and stories are an attempt to express some personal feelings about books that have impacted my life and, I believe, through me, the lives of others. We are the books we have read, the books that have been read to us. Those books mark each of us in special ways. To understand better what I mean, I turn to authors of two of my classics. Newberry award winner, Bill Armstrong, author of *Sounder*, writes in the prologue to his book:

The world of long ago has almost totally
changed. The church balcony is gone. The
table is gone from the kitchen. But the story
remains.[1]

Diane Wolkstein, in the last few pages of the Chinese tale *White Wave*, writes:

When the old man died, the shell was lost.
In time, the shrine, too, disappeared. All
that remained was the story. But that is how
it is with all of us: When we die, all that
remains is the story.[2]

Over time, people die, and much disappears—yet, they remain alive through their stories. What will be your story carried by the children, the bridge-kids, and the young adults that you have taught—whose lives you have touched? What story of you will remain?

I have been asked what I want carved on my headstone. I think I would like it to read,

Here lies Cherie Clodfelter; her story remains

But when even that headstone disappears, I hope that I remain through my story.

Notes

1 Armstrong, William H. *Sounder*. Harper & Row, 1969.
2 Wolkstein, Diane. *White Wave*. Thomas Y. Crowell, 1979.

Friends Offer Tribute

to

Cherie A. Clodfelter, Ph.D.

teacher, colleague, friend

University of Dallas Piper Professors (clockwise from top): Richard P. Olenick, Physics; Frank J. Doe, Biology; Cherie A. Clodfelter, Education; Louise S. Cowan, English; Judith A. Kelly, Drama

Cherie A. Clodfelter & Ashley Bryan

Tribute from Ashley Bryan

Dr. Cherie Clodfelter leads her students to an exciting adventure in the world of art and literature. The original work produced by her students attests to the wisdom of her direction.

Dr. Clodfelter's intellectual curiosity is so disarming that she captures your heart immediately. Her students work in class as a family, enjoying challenges in literature that open to ongoing personal discoveries.

Dr. Clodfelter is an inspired educator whose example urges her students to a lifelong commitment to growth in learning and sharing.

BRAVO, Dear Friend!

(Editor's note: Ashley Bryan is the illustrator or author of more than 30 books for children. He has known Dr. Clodfelter for many, many years and has made numerous visits to her Child and Young Adult Literature class at the University of Dallas as part of the Authors, Illustrators, and Illustrators (A.I.R.) program. His awards and honors include the Coretta Scott King Award for illustration, six Coretta Scott King Honor awards, the Arbuthnot Prize, and a Fulbright Scholarship. A former teacher at Dartmouth College, he has compiled, written, and illustrated numerous books, many of them based on African folk tales.)

Louise Cowan & Cherie A. Clodfelter

Tribute from Dr. Louise Cowan

Cherie Clodfelter has numerous achievements of which she can be justly proud. She has won awards, written articles, designed curricula, delivered public lectures, attended conferences, and participated in civic organizations. But above all else, Dr. Clodfelter is a teacher. Her entire life has been spent witnessing to a love of learning. She has shared this love with hundreds of students in a long career as college professor and has gone one step further. She has taught students to disseminate the joy and excitement of learning. She knows that the world moves forward by one generation helping the next to acquire knowledge--and she is convinced that the art of providing that help must itself be taught. Her life, therefore, has been spent in teaching teachers. Her pupils head classrooms not only in the Dallas-Fort Worth area but throughout the nation.

Dr. Clodfelter's remarkable achievement has not been limited to teaching, however, but extended to curriculum design as well. As Chairman of the Education Department at the University of Dallas, she has designed a program that, in accommodating a demanding core curriculum, has had to deepen and intensify its professional courses. They have been made sufficiently inclusive to give education majors a sound disciplinary foundation while allowing the diversity of the liberal arts. Like all the other students at UD, those majoring in education fulfill their science, math, history, art, and foreign language requirements, read the philosophic, theological, and literary texts that have shaped the West, and—most of them—spend a semester on the UD Rome campus, studying the classics with their friends. UD education majors are thus distinguished by the breadth of their liberal learning, with a very different preparation from that offered in most colleges and universities. They could perhaps be called unique in today's world, with a remarkable knowledge of the ideas that have shaped our culture. Yet Dr. Clodfelter has made sure at the same time that their mastery of their professional work is superior.

But she has sponsored no particular method, no arcane psychological scheme. Cherie Clodfelter fosters no hard and fast rules for teaching. She has a favorite anecdote about a boy who in a very brief time has taught his dog to obey some difficult commands. When he's asked what his secret is, he replies simply, "I know what I want him to learn—and I know my dog." And it is this knowledge of both one's material and one's students, this certainty that knowledge is conveyable, that has spelled the secret of Dr. Clodfelter's own success. She has been not only a teacher, but a mentor and a guide to her pupils, who trust her because she knows not only what needs to be taught but also the hearts and minds of her students, their secret desire to be transformed, so that they may carry to others the keys to knowledge.

Her students have one further advantage over most other aspiring young would-be teachers. They have studied children's literature with Cherie Clodfelter, a national authority on the subject. And in so doing, they have had their imaginations awakened and their sensitivity enhanced. In directing her students to reanimate their childhood imaginations, Dr. Clodfelter has provided access to the eternal world of magic and delight. What tribute can be paid to someone who has opened up an endless source of transformation and wonder? "Clodfelter's Classics" stay with her pupils over the years, not only as guide to the depth and range of the child's imagination but as testimony to the eternal youth of the human spirit.

Cherie Clodfelter's students know in their hearts that teaching involves a kind of alchemy. Their desire to work a magical transformation in the world has led them, in fact, to become education majors. But Dr. Clodfelter has seen to it that her students acquire something more even than a broad liberal education; they acquire a habitus, a habit of soul that becomes their most precious possession. They are teachers. Their dispositions are shaped by this inner strength, whatever they may do in life. They have been given not only a glimpse of the good but a desire to share it, to lead others to it. Throughout life, like the souls in Dante's Purgatorio, who joyously welcome newcomers to their group, they will be inclined to say: Here are others with whom we may share our knowledge

Over the years Cherie Clodfelter has given so much of herself in her relations with students that one wonders how there will be anything left of her to retire. And besides, what will she do in those Colorado mountains where she plans to make her home after leaving UD? Will she, like Annie Dillard, teach the stones—and the bears and the wolves—to talk? Or, like St. Francis, will she preach to the birds? And tell them stories? It is hard to imagine otherwise, for teaching is her posture, her attitude toward life, her calling. And her influence will go on in the world, transmitted by the hundreds of young people she has taught.

Aristotle declared teaching to require the highest kind of knowledge, since to teach something, one must be able to explain it and hence must understand its essentials, with a far higher knowledge of it than ordinary. Thus the teacher is not a mere expert in technique, but a pursuer of wisdom. But, alas, the profession is hardly regarded in that manner today. The general decline of respect for teachers in our time has resulted in an educational expertism, in which the work of teachers, like their preparations for their careers, is quantified, becoming something that can be mastered, like a skill or a technique. This attempt to make the discipline into a kind of pseudo-science has had disastrous effects on its actual pedagogy. Thus to go against the general trend by approaching education as one of the liberal arts is to turn away from its behavioral principles toward the less measurable qualities that mark true learning in the other disciplines. This is no doubt the way education programs will go in the near future; but it has been Cherie Clodfelter's distinction—and the mark of her courage—to lead the way toward this humanization of her discipline.

(Editor's Note: Dr. Louise Cowan is Professor Emeritus, University of Dallas, a colleague, and friend to Dr. Clodfelter. She received her Ph.D. in 1953 from Vanderbilt University. She served for many years as the Graduate Dean and Chair of the English Department at the University of Dallas, and as Director of its Institute of Philosophic Studies. With her husband, Dr. Donald Cowan, she pioneered the University's core curriculum based on classic texts. She is a Founding Fellow of the Dallas Institute of Humanities and Culture, and the recipient of numerous awards, grants, and professorships, including the National Endowment for the Humanities' Charles Frankel Prize for her work in advancing the study of the humanities. Dr. Cowan's publications include The Fugitive Group (LSU Press, 1959), The Southern Critics (University of Dallas Press, 1971), The Terrain of Comedy, ed. (Dallas Institute, 1984), Teaching the Teachers (1986), The Epic Cosmos, ed. with Larry Allums (Dallas Institute, 1992), Classic Texts and the Nature of Authority, ed. with Donald Cowan (Dallas Institute, 1993), and, most recently, Invitation to the Classics (Baker Book House, 1998), ed. with Os Guinness. In addition, she has published numerous articles on Faulkner, Coleridge, Homer, Aristophanes, Shakespeare, Eudora Welty, Toni Morrison, and others.)

The Clodfelter Impact:
"A Model to Emulate..."
What Students Say

Colleagues, friends, and former students toast Dr. Cherie A. Clodfelter at her April 2007 retirement gala.

Affecting Eternity: A Lifetime of Contribution
From Barbara Khirallah, editor

Over thirty years ago, my teacher was a black-haired woman who read stories.

"TERRIFIC PIG!" I listened as Charlotte lovingly wove her web for Wilbur, giving of herself, sacrificing much to give him life.

When I heard that Sounder's master had disappeared, I understood that boy, who in his lonely searching retold "the stories his mother had told him at night in the cabin, the stories that he asked her to tell him over and over because he liked the way they always ended with the right thing happening . . . with people in stories who never feared of anything."

Like that boy, I found comfort in knowing and telling the stories, the stories of Ramona and Joshua T. Bates and Obadiah and Margaret, who had that special relationship with God.

And, like Alexander, when I was having a *Terrible, Horrible, No Good, Very Bad Day,* I made plans. I made plans for all that I would be and do in this life, no matter what. When my teacher read about Mrs. Mallard who led her ducklings through the streets of Boston in search of a proper home, she led me. She led me through the stories of my childhood in search of the teacher she wanted me to find in myself.

This black-haired, wide-eyed, passionate woman stood before me—all five feet of her. She planted in me a seed, and she showed me what the flower could look like. She made me struggle, she made me risk, she made me responsible, she made me dream—she made me want to know more and more and more.

My teacher was an Oklahoma girl, born in Bartlesville, and schooled in Dewey. In the third grade, Miss Emorine Williams told her, "Learning is never easy, Cherie Ann. (They all had double names in Oklahoma.) It is the struggle that makes you feel good that you have learned." In the seventh grade, Mr. Thomas Reynolds, as burly as a grizzly bear, called all of his students by their last names. "Clodfelter, you are responsible for your learning," he told her. "The more you learn, the more you want and need to learn. Learning is an incurable disease, and I'm here to see that you don't find a cure!" In high school, Mr. Bernard Mitchell "was so short and so dreamy," she once told us, her students. "I knew he liked me, and I wouldn't have disappointed him for the world." He was the one who explained to her, "Science is a way of knowing so that you can make predictions about what should be known. The art of science is the risk and the dream."

Cherie A. Clodfelter became the master artist—perfecting the risk to achieve her dream.

Cherie Ann finished high school at the tender age of sixteen—even back then she liked to get things done way ahead of schedule. She attended Oklahoma State University, where she was a cheerleader and a golf champion. To this day, one can find her cheering for Oklahoma State as well as the Dallas Cowboys in the Braniff Building, downstairs in the "foundation" of the University. She earned her degree at OSU in education and in earth science.

After college, Cherie came to Irving, Texas, where her parents had moved. She had suffered a tragic loss in her life, and so she came "home" to family. She began teaching in the Irving Independent School District as an elementary school teacher. (She also taught geology and astronomy at the local high school on a part-time basis.) For the next few years during the day, she taught at Britain, Farine, and Brandenburg Elementary Schools. At night and during summers, she worked on her master's degree. Upon completion of her degree, she was invited to read her thesis in Chicago, at the national conference of the National Association for Research in Science. From 1969 to 1970, Cherie completed an internship at the Center for Applied

Linguistics at George Washington University. She also worked that year on a National Science Foundation Grant with the University of Nebraska.

In 1970, Cherie was teaching second grade at Brandenburg Elementary when Dr. Donald Cowan, President of the University of Dallas, called with an invitation to join the Department of Education faculty. As was her style, Cherie took the risk—and the job!

In 1974, Cherie had earned her PhD from Texas Woman's University. That same year, she served as senior author for an eighteen-volume reading basal series with Harper and Row. That series was adopted in forty-nine states. Also in 1974, Cherie Clodfelter, PhD became the Chairman of the Department of Education, a post she held until her retirement in June 2007.

During her years of service at the University of Dallas, Cherie represented the university well. She maintained professional memberships with a host of organizations at the city, state, national, and international levels. Many times, she served as a keynote speaker at various professional conferences where her presentations were always well received. Her continuing work with the International Reading Association, American Library Association, Kappa Delta Pi, North Texas Reading Council, Society of Children's Book Writers, Irving Independent School District, Dioceses of Dallas and Fort Worth, and Irving Chamber of Commerce, to mention just a few of the organizations that she served, brought honor and distinction to the University and the Department of Education.

Cherie built a solid reputation for excellence in education. Her mastery in the classroom rested upon an insatiable desire to know more, to do more, to see more, and to be more. After Cherie hired me to teach in the Department of Education in 1992, I began to understand more and more the impact of this one small woman. Whenever I visited a student teacher, attended a professional meeting, or simply sat in a classroom, if I mentioned that I taught at the University of Dallas, people always reacted: "Teachers that come of your program are always well prepared to be teachers. Cherie Clodfelter knows what good teachers are, what they do!"

Cherie's professional awards and contributions are so numerous that it is impossible to name them all. However, there are a few that stand out. In 1986, her colleagues at the University of Dallas selected her as their King Fellow for significant scholarly contributions and for exemplifying the "qualities of a teacher, colleague, and scholar at the University". Since that year, an anonymous donation made to honor her excellence in teaching has brought educators of national reputation to campus as part of the Excellence in Education Forum. In 1988, the International Reading Association recognized her with their Honor Award for Teaching. Also, she has been named to the White Rose Circle of Kappa Delta Social Fraternity and inducted into the Texas Hall of Fame.

The Cherie A. Clodfelter Children's Literature Library, named in her honor, is located in the Department of Education at the University of Dallas. It is filled completely with books sent to Cherie for review by publishers, authors, and editors. Even today, after retirement from the university, she continues to review books and contribute to professional journals so that publishers will continue to send newly published children's books to "her" library. In addition, she continues to participate with *Authors, Illustrators, and Readers* (A.I.R.), a collaborative project that she developed with the Irving Independent School District and the Irving Public Library to introduce notable children's book authors and illustrators to students each year.

For all of her many contributions, perhaps Cherie's most notable contribution—the one for which she will always be remembered —is her uniquely personal gift for ***inspiring*** and ***supporting*** us as teachers, readers, and learners as we discover and rediscover the joy, reward, and value of creating and sharing good child and young adult literature. To this end, each semester in her Child and Young Adult Literature course, Cherie read to her students. She read orally each class day without fail and demanded that her students read aloud as well. Later, after they had become teachers with their own classrooms, she checked to make sure that they were reading to their own students. In addition, she required her students to build anthologies of "classic" children's literature and to write and self-publish a child or young adult book. To recognize the quality of the literature published, the Clodecott Award was established. Each year an engraved medallion is presented to the author/illustrator of the best children's book written in the Child and Young Adult Literature course. The name of the award comes from blending the name of the award given by the American Library Association to honor the best picture book of the year for children—the Caldecott Award – with the name of Dr. Cherie Clodfelter.

In May 2007, Dr. Cherie A. Clodfelter retired from the University of Dallas. In April of that year, the University of Dallas hosted a spectacular gala to celebrate her many years of service. Hundreds of former students, colleagues, and friends attended the gala. Two major announcements were made that evening. First, the President of the University announced that Dr. Cherie A. Clodfelter had been selected by the Minnie Stevens Piper Foundation as a Piper Professor, a prestigious award for superior teaching at the college and university level in the State of Texas. Second, the Clodfelter Retirement Committee announced the future publication of this book, *Books that All Children Should Hear and Read: Perpetuating the Stories*.

Now a year later, the publication of this book is offered to you as a guide for discovering and rediscovering the joy, reward, and value of reading and sharing good child and young adult literature. May you find in these pages the inspiration that comes from the passion of my friend Cherie Clodfelter and honor her legacy by *Books that All Children Should Hear and Read: Perpetuating the Stories*.

Tribute to My Teacher
From Terri Gorton Fullerton

"What If . . ."

What if Cherie was a rock?
Layers of sediment
A mineral mosaic
Solidified into a distinct structure.
Was she changed by pressure?
Weathered by storms and struggles?

Time not fathomable
To create our rock
Unearthed for today's celebration.

Intersections of past and present
Embodiment of earth stories
A geological wonder,
Distinct from all other rocks.

People look all over the world
for this rock.
Its treasure lies within.
Once broken we see
an internal city.

Your true self revealed—
a work of God in nature.

Crystal citadels
Protrude beauty.
A community of translucent structures
Glittering wealth within
Reflecting heavenly sparkles

You, Cherie, are a geode
Which enables you
To see the geode in others—
Treasures sometimes beneath
Rough, hard surfaces.

What if Cherie was a book?

Between covers
That fit in your hands just right—

Her story grabs your attention
And pulls you into a text
Into a relationship
Author and reader
Professor and student
Colleague and friend.

Her story unites us
In the pages
Of our imagination.

Her story will become
Part of you.
You will become part of the greater story—
The quest of human nature.

(Editor's note: Terri Gorton Fullerton graduated from the University of Dallas in 1987. Her suggestion to Dr. Clodfelter while she was enrolled in the Child and Young Adult Literature class resulted in the establishment of the Clodecott Award, an engraved medallion presented each year to the author/illustrator of the best children's book written in the Child and Young Adult Literature class. The name of the award comes from blending the name of the award given by the American Library Association to honor the best picture book of the year for children—the Caldecott Award—with the name, Dr. Cherie Clodfelter, Professor of Education, who taught Child and Young Adult Literature at the University of Dallas from 1970–2007. The Clodecott Award winner is announced at an annual reception in the Department of Education.)

From Students

News traveled fast among those taking education courses back in 1971. "Good Lord, a second-grade teacher is coming to teach at UD! Oh, she ought to be a real REAL challenge!" "Well, this will be an easy A!" "Do you think she can read cursive?" For over thirty years, UD students have talked about her, dreamed with her, and learned from her.

They explain her impact in their own words:

"I hope you know that you were and are an important role model in my life."

—Rita Laws '76

"All that I learned and practiced in Education at the University has stood me well. . . . Here's hoping that you stay another twenty-five years, since I'm hoping Brian will want to go there in a few years. He thinks he wants to be a teacher, too, you know—to study that old incunabula. It's funny, the things you don't forget."

—David C. Corbett '88

"I will never forget my first week of classes at UD so many years ago. That first day, I attended Introduction to Philosophy, Literary Traditions I, and Art History. I left each of them feeling like I was in way over my head and that I was attending the wrong university. On my second day of school, I attended your practicum course. There you stood, a dynamic woman, whose energy and enthusiasm for teaching and love of her students made me realize I had chosen to attend the right university."

—Mary Jo Lemming Gorcyca '78

"In your next twenty-five years, I hope to sit in your class again."
—Jackie Lancaster Greenfield '72

"You were a great role model to me of what a strong woman is and how a strong woman carries herself.

—Catherine Sauer '87

"Thank you for having taught me. Thank you for having argued with me."

—Mary Ann Hyde '72

"I want you to know that barely a day goes by when I don't find myself thinking of you."

—Joe Clary

"The quick brown fox jumps over the lazy dog…ah the memories."

—Brigid Binder Novacek '94, Maureen Binder '95

"I like coming to the education department. It is not like any other department on this campus. Everyone is always laughing and talking, and all that stuff in the children's library reminds me of my room at home when I was a little kid."

—Lisa, UD student

"Mom, how does Dr. Clodfelter know so much?"

—David Khirallah, who said this while still a future UD student

"Once upon a time," Miss Huff explained, "is how to start a story." But, Cherie Ann knew that a story was *supposed* to start, "when I was a little boy. Even if I am not a little boy—that doesn't make any difference. It has to start that way." So said Cherie Ann to Miss Huff, "My daddy always starts his stories that way."

—Cherie Ann Clodfelter, age 8.

In Appreciation

I would like to offer special thanks to the many people who contributed time, talent, and resources to the publication of *Books that All Children Should Hear and Read: Perpetuating the Stories* and support for the Dr. Cherie A. Clodfelter Scholarship.

- Dr. Frank Lazarus, President of the University of Dallas

- Mr. George Engdahl, Vice President, Office of Advancement

- Ms. Kay Haaser, Certification Officer in the Department of Education

- Dr. Richard Olenick, Chairman University of Dallas Physics Department

- Terri Randall, Administrative Assistant in the Department of Education

- Carol Little and members of the University of Dallas Office of Advancement

- Dr. Ron Clodfelter, Cherie's brother

- Mr. Cory Meiser, Director of film tribute to Dr. Clodfelter

- Elizabeth and Christina Leano, musicians

- Sybil Novinski, University historian

- Scott Dupree, Director of the University of Dallas Library

- Ms. Katherine Andrzejewski, student worker in the Department of Education of the University of Dallas

- Members of the Department of Education: Dr. Jerry Irons, Dr. Jo Ann Patton

- **Speakers at the Clodfelter Retirement Celebration**

  - Mary Bonness Hansell, UD class of 1981

  - Terri Gorton Fullerton, UD class of 1987

  - David Hicks, UD class of 1988

  - Amber Chesser, UD class of 2007

  - Susie Arnold, Administrative Assistant, Department. of Education (Retired)

  - Mary Lankford, Director Library Services, Irving ISD (Retired)

  - Dr. John Crain, former UD faculty, Department of Education

  - Dr. Richard P. Olenick, Chairman, UD Department of Physics

  - Barbara Khirallah, UD class of 1971, colleague, UD Department of Education

- All contributors to the Dr. Cherie A. Clodfelter Scholarship fund

–Barbara Khirallah, Editor

The Last Word
Barbara Khirallah, Editor

Cherie A. Clodfelter & Barbara Khirallah

*T*hirty-seven years ago, Dr. Cherie A. Clodfelter started a story at the University of Dallas. She began by planting a dream to grow teachers who serve as models for their students to emulate. For that dream, she risked everything. Over the years, she tilled, watered, and fed that dream until it generated seeds that grew into tiny buds, each needing its own time and special care to bloom. To nurture her garden, Dr. Clodfelter read to the tiny buds, sprinkling them with the stories that all the young should read and hear—stories of country, family, and love. She read to her tiny buds in a voice of determination and hope. As each tiny bud bloomed, it became part of a magnificent garden of teachers, each of whom carried the voice of a hardy, life-giving dream. From meager beginnings, a single, feisty, little gardener planted a single dream which bloomed and regenerated itself in classrooms everywhere. As William Armstrong, author of *Sounder*, one of the many well-loved stories that Dr. Clodfelter read to her tiny buds, wrote, "If a flower blooms once, it goes on blooming somewhere forever. It blooms on for whoever has seen it blooming." I was one of the seeds generated in Dr. Clodfelter's garden, and I have seen her dream bloom. I know the voice and the stories that she offered me. Like all of the others that she has nurtured, I discovered my own voice to share the stories first with my students and then with my five children. I hope that you will also find your own voice with which to share the stories in *Books that All Children Should Hear and Read: Perpetuating the Stories*.

In April 2007, the University of Dallas hosted a celebration to honor Dr. Clodfelter for her thirty-seven years of committed service. Colleagues, friends, and former students from around the country gathered to honor this very short—but large in life—teacher. During the program, Dr. Frank Lazarus, President of the University of Dallas, announced with great pleasure that Dr. Clodfelter had been awarded a 2007 Minnie Stevens Piper Professor Award for superior teaching at a Texas college. Amidst the applause, I could only think how important it is that we continue to *hear her voice and perpetuate the stories.*

On a very personal note, Cherie, I know that you are most proud of the establishment of the Cherie A. Clodfelter Scholarship fund. You have given not only your life's work to the University of Dallas but now also your legacy. This book has been published to add to and support that legacy and to honor you as a teacher.

I love you—we all love you.

—Barbara Khirallah, Editor

Author Index

Curtis, Christopher Paul · 21
Curtis, Patricia · 40

D.
d'Aulaire, Ingri · 40, 54
d'Aulaire, Edgar Parin · 40, 54
dePaola, Tomie · 4
Di Camillo, Kate · 21
Dixon, Franklin W. · 25

F.
Fox, Paula · 22
Freedman, Russell · 41, 42
Fritz, Jean · 43

G.
Geisel, Theodore · 4
George, Jean · 22
Greene, Bette · 23
Grey, Zane · 23
Grimm, Jakob · 55
Grimm, Wilhelm · 55

H.
Henkes, Kevin · 5
Hinton, S. E. · 24
Howe, James · 24

J.
Jakes, John · 43
Jarrell, Randall · 56

K.
Keene, Carolyn · 25
Kitchen, Bert · 5
Konigsburg, E. L. · 25

Title Index

S.

T.

U.

W.

Ordering Information

To order this book, please visit
www.brownbooks.com.

Proceeds from the sale of this book support the
Dr. Cherie A. Clodfelter Scholarship fund.